SHINE

A HANDBOOK FOR LIVING

CASSANDRA WILCOX

Swallow Bridge Publishers
9 Upper Lodge Mews, Bushy Park,
Hampton Hill, Middlesex TW12 1NE

www.swallowbridge.com

© Cassandra Wilcox 2012
ISBN 978 0 957 1897 0 6

SHINE

A HANDBOOK FOR LIVING

For my babies,
and my babies' babies

CONTENTS

Believe nothing,
no matter where you read it
or who has said it, not even if
I have said it, unless it agrees
with your own reason and
your own common sense.

Buddha

INTRODUCTION

Our lives are made rich with stories. Stories help define our culture and beliefs, underscoring what is right and what is wrong. Be they holy texts, myths or fairytales, or present day reports that we watch on television or read in the newspapers, stories are woven into the fabric of our daily lives.

From a very young age, the experiences and actions of the stories' characters, real and fictional, good and bad, resonate with us, and from them we learn how to deal with our own experiences. We learn to avoid the villains – or becoming villainous ourselves. The victims teach us what might happen if we don't take care and responsibility for our actions. And through the heroes and heroines we connect to the person inside ourselves, and to our highest aspirations. They are who we can become, if we dare.

This book is written in two parts – one part, story and the other part, accompanying the story, fact. Two parts, two voices, one book.

There are two sides to everything, and at least two ways of dealing with every situation. There is your way – the way that feels familiar and right to you, and there is another way. It can be helpful, if a little uncomfortable, to sometimes think about the 'other way,' and consider how we – and others – might benefit if we were to change our thinking and repeated patterns of behaviour.

This is what this book aims to do: combining story and fact, it presents different perspectives on important issues that, at some point in our lives, affect us all.

Although the story is set in the 1980s – a decade of money, greed, lust for power and corporate rule, its themes are universal and the story, timeless.

It tells the tale of a young woman who travels to the other side of the world to make her dream come true. Following her journey, we join in her struggle to overcome the challenges that meet her – the challenges that meet all of us – along the way. Her story is our story. It's a story about striving to succeed against the odds. It's a story about friendship and separation. A story about pleasure, and the pain that always walks one step behind pleasure. A story about love lost and lessons found, and the importance of listening to your heart, and trusting your heart.

At every stage along her journey, we are reminded of what we already know but so often forget – that we always have a choice. Never is there only one way. Always is there another, sometimes better way.

But what is the better way? What is the wise way, the way that will bring us the elusive happiness we yearn for?

Accompanying the story is the factual part of the book, the part that contains words of wisdom from people, past and present, poignant and powerful passages and quotations that blend valuable advice and knowledge from ancient thinking with contemporary scientific discoveries.

Drawing on the insights and experiences of those whose lives inspire and guide us, we learn traditional simple values and remedies, as well as practical solutions for everyday living. The book asks, and attempts to answer those age old but important questions: Who am I? And where can I find the happiness I seek?

Through story and truth, the book reassures and reminds us that everyone is unique, and every life is special. And every dream can come true.

DREAM

In her twenty-second year she left England, just as her father had done before her. Unlike her father, she left by air, not sea, chartering her own course to a new destination, because if we didn't follow our own path we would never evolve, and neither would humanity. She arrived in Sydney late, too late to see the sun. It was midnight when she stepped out of the airport and boarded a bus to downtown Kings Cross. There, in the Bellevue Hostel, she lay on a bed in a small damp room unable to sleep.

Staring at the mould in the corner of the ceiling she closed her eyes and drifted into what felt like a drunken dream in which all sounds were coming from a kind of half distance, and were only half real. When she opened her eyes nothing had changed. The mould on the ceiling hadn't disappeared, nor had the old brown wardrobe with the door hinges held on with paperclips. She noticed that the peach coloured walls, also invaded by mould, bore the greasy marks of Blu-Tack, presumably the legacy of a previous guest who had tried to brighten up the room with pictures of white beaches and oceans blue.

As the night turned quickly to day her spirits lifted. 'I am in Australia,' she whispered to herself, feeling a sense of triumph at the thought. And she quickly added, before she forgot, the most important thought of all, 'and all my dreams will come true.'

She fumbled inside the bag on the floor beside her and retrieved a letter. No ordinary letter, it was written by a famous Australian film director. The first time she had read the letter was the time she knew for certain that her dream would come true. It was one of those green light, lottery-winning, turn your life around letters. The kind of letter that sends you out to buy a one-way ticket to Sydney. The letter was dated May 11th 1981. Handwritten by Ford Berry, it was short and to the point:

Dear Jem,

Thank you for your letter and CV. With your experience in television production, I'm sure you won't have any trouble making the transition into features. I have a couple of projects in the pipeline, and if you can get here before June, I'm sure I can give you a job. Call me when you arrive. F. B.

Today she would phone him and make an appointment to start her new life.

Brighton, she thought as the bus pulled away and she stood on Campbell Parade looking at a row of brightly coloured beach shops and cafes. Behind her, across the busy road was Bondi Beach. No, she changed her mind. Not Brighton, Littlehampton. With sunshine.

She was only partly right. Bondi, with its ice-cream cafes, postcards, souvenirs and fish and chips shops was indeed similar to Littlehampton but only because it's a seaside town. Beyond the signs for Cornettos and cappuccinos it bore little resemblance to anywhere in England.

A row of dishevelled 1950s buildings sat dwarfed by the ugly, high rise Cosmopolitan Inn. There was something sad and weary about the parade of shops staring blankly out to sea, as if they had seen too many late nights and hangovers and had themselves become a dull headache. It occurred to her that in the short time since she'd arrived, she was always comparing this place to where she had come from, and she resolved to try and stop as there was little point. The past was gone, the future didn't exist, all that mattered was now, and the only point worthy of comparison was the fact that the sun was shining.

It was, in part, her determination to follow

the sun that had led her here. Many years ago her mother, a wise and wonderful woman, had pointed her in the right direction. She vividly remembered the two of them lying on the grass in the garden of their small suburban London house, long after her father had died. The sun was streaming down on them and her mother's shining, luminous face revealed little sign of her advancing years. Instead, it had the same translucent quality you see in very young children. 'Follow the light, Jem,' her mother smiled at her as the sun bathed her soft, beautiful features. 'Turn your face to the sun.'

The girl did as her mother said. 'Close your eyes and imagine the sun's rays pouring into your heart and out again, and say: You, who are the giver of all life, light up my heart, light up my day, light up my life.' The girl closed her eyes and visualised the sun's rays pouring into her and repeated the words, and as she did so, she felt the sun's rays streaming into her and a physical surge of energy, like an electric current, piercing her heart and racing around her body and radiating out through her hands.

She opened her eyes to see her mother watching her with a smile that could light up the whole world. At that moment, the girl knew the sun would shine its light on the path she must follow, and illuminate her way.

The letter in her bag, and the visa in her passport were confirmation of this belief, that here in this faraway land where the sun always shined, her dream would come true. Never had this thought seemed more real than right now as she sat on the beach, curling her toes into the soft sand and staring out to sea, hypnotised by the haze of the Pacific Ocean.

Her dream was to write a film, not any film but a powerful, important film, one that people would talk about and remember. She had worked with film makers for many years, and all the time she had watched and listened and learned much, but as hard as she tried she had never found the opportunity to take the role she dreamed of.

Maybe there was too much competition, maybe the timing was always wrong. Maybe, she told herself many times, it was just not meant to be. But at other times she felt something stirring inside her that was too strong to be ignored. More than a desire, it was a compulsion, a physical need. And so she had followed that need to Australia, the country that was producing the most acclaimed films in the world, the land where you could be anything you wanted to be, and nothing and no-one could stop you.

This was her dream; to write, to create, to live a life in which the days melted into each other, and no minute of the day was spent wishing she were somewhere else. Maybe she would meet a man, a kind, strong and noble man. Maybe that was a dream too far, dependent as it was on fate.

Some people she regarded as friends called her dream naive, even impossible. But she chose to ignore their cynicism. Instead she held her dream close, imagining it in all its detail; the little weatherboard house in which she would live, worn by the wind and waves, its grey-white painted walls, the way the comfortable cushions on the old sofa sagged in the middle, the faded, pine kitchen table at which she would write and from which could look out of the window at the water, all the while the heat of the sun warming her bones, the stars firing her imagination. Her reverie was broken by squeals of laughter of two young women, running, laughing into the sea, arms waving, legs splashing. She watched them play and looked forward to the time when she would be that free.

Sydney, she quickly discovered, is the same size as London but with a third of the population. And though the city's public transport system is adequate, she knew that working on a feature film entailed predawn starts and early morning finishes. She also knew that, despite her limited budget, a car was a necessity not a luxury.

It was love at first sight. Like a rocket, the 1965 Ford Falcon shone out from the crowd of second-hand Japanese cars, its low-slung *American Graffiti* body and gleaming white bonnet stretching to infinity before her. But its most striking feature was on the front of the bonnet; the original chrome aeroplane shone, poised, ready for take off. She ran her fingers along the sharp pointed nose of the plane and it felt cool to touch. She climbed into the front bench seat. The red vinyl-clad interior was vast. From below the steering wheel, she flipped opened a rusty metal door through which she could see the ground below.

'Air conditioning,' piped up the young salesman with spiky blonde hair, as he peered through the driver's window, his face a little too close to hers. From below the dashboard she pulled out a handmade laminated tray with two round holes in it.

'Drinks holder – for yer tinnies,' the salesman shouted above the roar of a bus speeding along the Parramatta Road, 'for drive-ins. Youse bin to a drive-in?' If his question was an invitation, it was one she chose to ignore.

'What's the warranty on it?' she tried to sound like she knew what she talking about.

'Three months,' the young man replied. 'She's a bewdy,' he said looking at her as she walked around the car.

'Three months isn't very long,' she said, looking him straight in the eye.

'I could make it sex, I mean six.'

It wasn't until she was driving back to the city that she realised she was in trouble. She had never seen, let alone driven a car of that size or power, and when a truck came roaring past, she mounted the kerb in panic. If I don't kill someone by knocking them down, she thought, the plane will impale them for sure. With every ounce of concentration she gripped the steering wheel and realised, not too late, that if she could manage to keep the plane pointing in the middle of the lane it would guide her, like a compass, straight ahead.

Back at the hostel, her sense of accomplishment at having successfully driven – and parked – the Falcon, quickly turned to disappointment. There were no messages for her at reception, despite her having spoken twice with Mr Berry's secretary to organise her start date.

Sometimes when you're not sure what to do, events occur without forewarning but with a clear answer. Passing the doorway to the lounge, she was stopped by the rising volume of the television, and the sight of a small group of backpackers peering at the screen, listening intently to the news.

A train crash south of Sydney had killed 11 people and injured dozens more. At the end of the story the newsreader read out an emergency phone number for worried relatives to call before moving on to the next item: 'The Australian film industry suffered a severe blow today when Treasurer, John Howard, passed a law through parliament closing a tax loophole. Mr Howard's withdrawal of regulation 10BA that allows investors to place money, tax-free, into Australian films has sparked widespread anger in the industry...'

She stared at the screen in silent disbelief. One of the backpackers was speaking to her, but she didn't hear his words. As the enormity of the news began to sink in, she felt she might be sick. Suddenly, from seemingly nowhere, a quiet voice from inside her pierced her consciousness. It could be worse, she thought, I could have died in a train crash. Dazed, she walked out of the hostel into the daylight and turned her face to the sun.

DREAM

Of what do you dream? Do you dream of a life full of riches? Or a life rich with love? Do you dream of world peace? Or just more peace in your day? Do you dream of running your own business? Or running a marathon and crossing the finish line? Maybe you dream that when you look in the mirror you see a person looking back at you glowing with health and beauty. Or maybe you dream of living in a beautiful home filled with beautiful things. Perhaps you dream of living with less things and more time, time to be you, time to dream.

Do you dream of raising a family with someone you love, and who loves you? Do you dream of writing a song that everyone will sing? Or painting a picture that hangs in the world's greatest gallery? Do you dream of power and success that shows the world how good you are? Is that your dream? Or do you not care too much what the world thinks and wish only to be free to create whatever you want, without the approval of the world or anyone in it. Perhaps you dream of the comfort that comes from living a life more ordinary; a life – and lifestyle – far removed from those who yearn to be famous in a world where celebrity has become an ambition in itself.

Perhaps your dream is simple, you want only to be happy. Only it's not that simple. Peace and contentment might sound like the easiest thing to achieve, but they are so often the hardest.

Maybe you look at other people who seem to be living their dream, and wonder what it is about your luck, or your personality that constantly seems to miss out? Whilst it can appear that others have more fun or more comfort, the truth is that they probably look at others and feel the same. They, too, have their dreams.

We all dream. We all, at times, wish we had something else or were doing something else, going somewhere else or, perhaps the biggest dream of all, being someone else. You only need to look in the newspaper, or at the people around you, the president, the cleaner, the prima ballerina, the shopkeeper, the builder, the writer, the entrepreneur, the mother, father, doctor, teacher, bus driver – everyone has a dream. But not everyone's dream comes true.

Some people let their dreams wither and die. Perhaps they told someone of their dream and, in return for their honesty, they were laughed at or told to 'get real' or 'grow up.' It's very easy, especially when you are young, to believe what others tell you and stop believing in your dream.

Jesse Jackson, American civil rights activist said 'No one should negotiate their dreams. Dreams must be free to flee and fly high. No government, no legislature has a right to limit your dreams. You should never agree to surrender your dreams.' You can also include no parent, no partner, no peer has a right to limit your dream.

Standing on the shoulders of the civil rights victory in America, another man with a vision rose to the world stage in 2008. If Barack Obama was ever told that he didn't have a hope of becoming US President, he never let it stop him from following his dream. Nor did Obama expect anyone else to take responsibility for making his dream come true – a message he made clear in a speech he gave after winning the US election primaries in which he said 'Change will not come if we wait for some other person or some other time. We are the ones we have been waiting for. We are the change that we seek.'

Those who pour scorn over your dreams are often those who have let their own dreams die. They themselves are cut off from their deepest desires and divorced from their true talent. It's likely that they, too, had someone walk all over their dreams. And now they tell you that what you dream of is 'unreal' when in actual fact, it is they who are living a kind of half life, haunted by the dreams they never pursued, unable to fulfil their real potential, and become the person they were born to be.

If someone, anyone, tells you that what you want to do is impossible, too difficult or that you will never achieve it, ignore what they say.

People who do not follow their dreams can become irritable and depressed, even physically ill. The feeling that there's an empty hole in your soul can lead to all kinds of problems including addictions as a way to escape the pain of reality. That is why it is so important that you take your dream seriously, and follow your soul's passion. Discover what it is that makes your heart sing and your spirit soar – no matter how grand or how simple it is, find it, protect it, nurture it. And never let it go.

There is no greater joy in life than to live the dream that awakens your heart and stirs your spirit, and no greater sadness than to sacrifice your dream, to live a life far removed from the life you dream of, a life that kills your spirit. Even as children, we dream of living a life in which we feel alive and fulfilled.

You are never too old, and it is never too late to realise your dreams. You were born with a unique and precious talent that only you possess, and only you can manifest. There is no-one else in the world like you, and whether or not you know it, there is a reason why you are here, a reason for being. In India and other Eastern countries, they call this your dharma, your purpose in life. Some people call it your destiny. It is more than a career choice, it is your whole being – what you are meant to be, whether that's a loving mother or a famous neurosurgeon. But it matters not what it's called, only that you recognise that there is a very real and important need for you to awaken your special talent, your gift or quality – whatever it is that makes you, you. For, in the immortal words of cartoon character Charlie Brown's best friend and child prodigy, Linus, 'There is no heavier burden than a great potential.'

In fact, your task may not be what you do at all, but what you are. It may be that you need to bring a virtue like patience, compassion or gentleness into your relationships with others. This way, you live by example, and the value of this is immeasurable.

Think, for a moment, about the people you loved who are no longer with you. Invariably, the people you miss the most are those who gave you not money, but something far more precious; they touched your life in a way that is meaningful. These people embody a special quality that sets them apart from all others – the grandfather who showed endless patience, the trusted friend who never let you down, the mother whose generosity was boundless. Too often we judge people by what they have achieved in material terms instead of what special quality they have that helps us grow. Someone once said that 'the purpose of life is to matter – to count, to stand for something, to have it make some difference that we lived at all.' When you show others the true meaning of kindness, optimism, compassion, respect, indeed any virtue, you make a real difference.

But what if you don't have a dream to follow? Or what if you have many dreams and are unsure which one is right? We live in a fast-paced, high-powered world where everyone seems to be chasing money and wanting tangible evidence of success, and it's easy to get confused. If you don't know what it is you wish for, or if you're unsure if your dream is your true destiny, be patient. The answer will come.

Ask yourself first, what inspires you and what you enjoy doing. Do you love being with children?

Do you like to get lost in making music? Do you feel good when you make a big sale? Then ask yourself, 'Does this benefit others?' It's important that what you do helps others in some way or, at the very least, causes no harm. This doesn't mean you need to become a volunteer aid worker in some war-torn country (although this is an incredible dream to follow), it simply means your dream must not be damaging to others. Maybe you dream of being a good friend to others. Or cooking good food that brings pleasure to many. Or maybe your dream is to build a business that creates jobs for people, and plenty of profit for you.

It makes no difference if you dream of winning an Olympic gold medal, or losing a few kilos, not if it's a big dream or little dream – if you can dream it, you can do it. And when you do it, when you pour your energy into something you create from your heart, it becomes a very powerful thing. HRH Prince of Wales echoed this belief when he said 'When you garden from your dreams, it's amazing the effect it has on everyone.'

How do you know if your dream is the right dream to follow? You will know because when you do what it is you want to do, you will lose track of time. The clock will tick faster, an hour will pass like a minute. You will feel energised, light and alive. You will want to get out of bed in the morning, and move closer to the person you are meant to be.

Another question you can ask yourself is 'if money and time were not an issue, what would I be doing?' If your answer is what you are already doing, then you are living your dream.

What is the difference between people who dream and those who are living their dreams? Courage. Your dream can and will come true, but only if you have the courage to pursue it. The Roman philosopher, Seneca said 'It is not because things are difficult that we do not dare. It is because we do not dare that things are difficult.'

The important question then is not, of what do you dream? But, do you dare to make your dream come true?

BELIEVE

There were only a handful of film producers in Sydney to call, and she'd called them all. Across the city, productions folded overnight. It was the same story in Melbourne. 'Post us your details and we'll keep them on file.' Or 'Call back in a couple of months when things have settled down.' She didn't have a couple of months.

With a street directory in her bag, along with a copy of her CV and an umbrella (for even in lands where dreams come true, it rains), she strode purposefully through the city.

The two bus drivers walking in front of her were oblivious to her eavesdropping, their steel ticket machines swinging from their shoulders, their uniform long white socks and sandals looking old fashioned and out of place on what had turned out to be a hot, humid day.

'So what d'you do on yer holidays?'

'Nothin'. Got drunk. Stayed drunk.'

They fell into a bored silence as she followed them, down George Street past the sandstone Bank of New South Wales building, its neoclassical columns bearing down on the pedestrians below. She was thankful that

Sydney's business district was so easy to navigate, laid out in a grid system with the major streets named after British Prime Ministers and Heads of State – George Street, Pitt Street, and Elizabeth Street running lengthways, intersected with smaller, less salubrious sounding streets; Barrack Street and Market Street leading into Chinatown. Here, above the Red Dragon restaurant and rows of orange dead ducks hanging in the window, was Dalldibs Day Media Agency, and the indomitable, chain-smoking Kerry Dalldibs.

'It's a quiet time of year, not a lot of movement, but we do have one or two interesting things.' Kerry pulled out a card from the index box on her desk and read out the details, 'Independent TV production company wants a junior secretary, filing, typing, answering the phone, that sort of thing.'

She was desperate, but with five years solid secretarial experience, not that desperate. She recalled the bus driver whose days were so uninspiring that, even on holiday, he obliterated them with alcohol.

'I'm not sure,' she ventured. 'It could be a bit of a backward step'.

Kerry lit another cigarette, 'Your choice,' she replied curtly, failing to conceal her disapproval. She felt that Kerry knew something that she did not and that she was caught up in a sequence of events over which she had little control. Her mother, who at this moment seemed very far away, had always instructed her to never forget that she always had a choice. In life, in love, in everything she did and every decision she made. It was this thinking that encouraged her to travel to the other side of the world to follow her dreams. 'Don't ever think you don't have a choice, you always have a choice, Jem.' Her mother's voice rang clear and loud in her mind. When she asked her mother how would she know what the right choice was, her mother replied that her heart would tell her, and to listen to her heart because it never lied. But right now her heart was silent, and her dreams felt like the dreams of a foolish girl with too much imagination, and too little luck. She started to bite a fingernail and quickly stopped herself. It was a habit she found impossible to break. For though she was as practical as she was a dreamer, she was also inclined to worry, as evidenced by her bitten nails. She sat on her hands to avoid embarrassment.

'Is there anything else?' she asked.

Kerry blew smoke across the desk as she flicked through the cards. 'Oh, we've just taken a creative secretary job for Dermot, McMasters and

Mills advertising agency in North Sydney, but no, you don't want advertising.'

No, she didn't want to work in advertising. The very idea of it filled her with disappointment. Advertising, she believed, was full of people whose superiority complexes were matched only by their salaries. Advertising was false. It was a lie. Film was the only true creative profession, in which people worked for a love of art not money. She had not travelled across the world to work in an advertising agency as a creative secretary. And what was a creative secretary exactly? How creative could a secretary be?

'North Sydney?' she enquired. Kerry answered the ringing phone on her desk and nodded, smiling.

The reception area was pink. Not a soft pastel pink but a lurid neon pink. Pink sofa, pink armchair next to a pink metal bubble gum machine full of pink bubble gums. Gold framed certificates alongside gleaming gold statues lined the pink painted walls on which big brass letters read Dermot, McMasters and Mills. She was, predictably, early for her first day. She stared down at her hands. And then she heard him, his loud, unmistakably Australian voice booming down the corridor, shouting at the receptionist. 'Who parked that bloody bomb in the car park? Get rid of it now!' Bob Wilson, Creative Director of Dermot, McMasters and Mills was a big man, tall and fat, who always had a huge cigar in his mouth, even when he was talking. 'Alright?' he looked at her as she rose to shake hands. 'Bob, but you can call me Boss.' He didn't smile, he chewed on his unlit cigar and stared at her, before turning and walking away. She followed him along the corridor, glancing through the glass walls into offices with desks that looked out through windows with views of the most beautiful harbour in the world.

She'd met his type before, bullish, brash and full of himself. In the face of his audacity, any nervousness she felt, disappeared. He led her into a corner office that boasted an even bigger view of the harbour and kicked a footstool in her direction, pointing at her to sit on it. He lit the cigar hanging from his fat mouth and his beady eyes narrowed at her. 'You know the drill. My jobs come first, use whatever brain you've got in that pretty little head and if you've got problems, I don't want to know. Alright?' She loathed his patronising tone, 'pretty little head?' Last time she looked, her head was neither pretty nor little. Like most young women she didn't consider herself especially attractive. Her nose was too big, her forehead too high, her hair, which she liked to keep big and messy in keeping with the fashion, was too wild. Only her eyes, pale green, the colour of spring, did she consider interesting, some would say arresting. If the eyes are the window of the soul, Jem's eyes spoke volumes.

She was shown to her desk outside his office from which she had a view of the corridor. On the desk was a phone, a pink IBM Golfball typewriter and a small pile of handwritten scripts. She sat down, opened a drawer, took out some blank script paper and started typing.

The days turned into weeks. With a small but regular income, she was able to find a place to live, a large bedsitting room in a 1920s red brick building in the faded but gracious, leafy harbourside village of Kirribilli, walking distance from the agency. The building was located next to a small parade of shops that she would rush past, only ever stopping at Miguel's Convenience Store, the ubiquitous corner store that was always stacked to the ceiling with all the things you could ever want and those you never knew you needed.

Though her room looked tired, it was perfect. Located on the third and top floor with no lift, it contained an eclectic mix of furniture that had served generations of tenants. In one corner was a kitchen area partitioned from the rest of the room by what looked like an old hospital screen. The remaining space was dominated by an enormous sofa bed that faced a pair of French doors leading onto a partly enclosed balcony from which she could see, across the freeway, the tower blocks of North Sydney. Far from the view – or the home – of her dreams, it was, she told herself, what she needed right now and she decided that she would paint the whole place white, the colour of purity and innocence.

From her room, a door led to the shameful excuse for a bathroom that was redeemed only by the fact that when she stood in the discoloured bath under the rusting showerhead she could see through the leadlight window, beyond the bell tower of the chapel of Loreto Convent, to a part of Sydney Harbour that was home to the Royal Australian Navy. Some mornings as she showered, she could glimpse the outline of a submarine half submerged, or catch the shimmering light of the sail of a yacht gliding past in the background.

She very soon discovered that she loved the harbour more than the beaches. There was something mysterious and melancholic about the harbour that suited her nature more that the blinding light and heat of the beach. The waterways of the harbour were not constant, they changed with your mood, and your mood changed with the harbour. It had numerous hidden bays and coves, each different from the last, and on weekends she made it her mission to either drive or take a ferry to a new location on the map: Lavender Bay, Kissing Point, Greenwich, Old Cremorne, Rose Bay, Birchgrove. This way, she learned to know Sydney, or at least its harbour, and very soon learned to love it.

'...I love the light, the colour' she wrote to her mother, *'the way the sky is so blue and so endless. I love the energy of the city when the sun shines, and the way it behaves like a child, naturally playful with an innocence that doesn't know the meaning of the word 'no'. I love the harbourside parks, the ones the tourists don't know – Elkington Park and Long Nose Point where every view is different yet familiar. I love that I can swim in North Sydney in an Olympic pool under the mile high arches of steel of the Harbour Bridge towering above me. I love the fact that Sydney thinks it's new but it's entrenched in tradition, with scones and tea served in the Art Deco city cafes, and women wearing*

white gloves who serve in the department stores where fashions are at least a year behind London. I love the jacaranda trees with purple blossoms that you glimpse on the lower north shore when you drive across the northern end of the bridge. I love sitting by the harbour at night listening to the chinking noise of the yachts. And I love the way the water changes colour from turquoise to royal blue to moody green to grey to midnight black. They say that America is the land of opportunity, but I think it's Australia.'

It was true, she did love Sydney. She just hated her job. Working in the creative department at Dermot, McMasters and Mills, or The Mill as it was called by those who worked there, was like working in a kindergarten. Grown men – and they were all men – played on the pinball machine or pool table in the games room of the creative department, only returning to their desks to 'create' after a long lunch at one of the local Asian restaurants. The copywriters and art directors were friendly enough, and often invited her to join them but on her wage, she couldn't afford to do that.

At the end of her working day, she'd walk

home down the hill towards the harbour and under the Harbour Bridge and along the water's edge, taking in the cool and cleansing breeze that blew in from the Pacific Ocean. Most evenings, she would stop to buy dinner in the form of a home-cooked takeaway meal from Miguel's corner store which was run by a hard-working, immigrant Portugese family, presided over by the matriarchal Theresa who, she discovered to her delight, prepared and sold delicious food at bargain prices; spinach and ricotta pie, olives stuffed with jalapeño peppers, crusty hard bread that filled her up for little cost, and on pay day, Peri Peri chicken.

There was always a queue for Theresa's dinners and always words of maternal advice in broken English offered freely. Theresa's head for business was as hard as her heart was soft. It was Theresa's business, she reckoned, to know everyone's business, ostensibly to provide a more personal service. 'Why you live in those no good flats?' Theresa demanded an answer from Jem. 'Why you not live in nice suburb? You work, you earn money?'

'I like it here, I can walk to work.'

'You need nice man, settle in, my Miggi is good boy, he look after you.'

Jem laughed and stopped herself when, right

on cue, Theresa's olive skinned, dark haired son walked into the shop and almost knocked her over with his surfboard before mumbling an apology and planting a dutiful kiss on top of his mother's head. Jem thought it an unusual display of affection for a young man, but then this was no usual Australian family. 'You want nice house in suburb,' Theresa continued as she reached for a takeaway food container into which she spooned a large portion of her homemade fish soup, 'You nice girl, you like nice house.'

She thanked Theresa for her dinner and, feeling better about herself, took her warm meal a few doors down, into the block where she lived and up the three flights of stairs to her room.

Most evenings she spent the same way, home alone, reading. Sometimes she would play a cassette of her favourite music on the portable tape player she had brought from England. If she'd had a good day, she would turn the volume up loud, and dance. The music would take her to a place that was in another world; a natural and wild place of beauty, a deeply intuitive and private place. Spinning round like a dervish, the music became her and she became the music. She danced without form but with such grace and fluidity it was mesmerising to watch, not that anyone ever watched her dance. She danced only for herself, an expression of the person no-one ever saw or knew. In the solitude of her room, these evenings were her release from all her worries, and her dancing, far from pointless, helped to sustain her spirit at a time when nothing was certain.

Her mornings, in contrast, had become predictable and dull. Boss would dictate letters to her, after which she'd make coffee for the creative teams who never arrived at work before ten o'clock and always with hangovers. Late in the afternoon their handwritten scripts would land on her desk for her to type. Scripts for television commercials, radio commercials and print ads for clients including a large brewery, pharmaceutical company and other multinationals. Big names, big budgets. Small ideas. There was no end of testimonial commercials featuring a new mum praising a new brand of nappies, or a young woman insisting that Brand X lotion was the only one that 'left my skin – and me – glowing!' One copywriter and art director team worked only on beer commercials. Lauded by their peers, their latest effort had the singular creative idea of a bunch of Australian cricketers getting drunk on cans of bitter after winning a match.

Her long working days were made longer by

endless empty hours in which she'd stare into the space of the corridor and wonder if she'd made the right choice or, indeed, what other choice she could make. It was not that her dream of writing a film was forgotten. It was that she now couldn't see a way to make it real. 'If you're climbing up a mountain and keep getting blocked maybe you need to try a different way,' her mother had suggested in one of their weekly telephone calls. But what other way was there? The harder she thought for an answer, the more the answer eluded her.

'What do you think of it?' a man's voice jolted her back into reality. Michael, a junior art director was standing next to her, reading the television script she'd just typed for the launch of a new drinking yoghurt. She was taken aback, no-one had ever asked her opinion on their work. Her response was diplomatic. 'I think it's…interesting, it's different.'

Michael grinned. 'Different is good, it's got to be different.' And he walked back into his office pleased with his work.

Although she agreed that a commercial – just like a film – needed to be different to have any impact, she also believed that it had to touch you in some way, and that you had to relate to it. Michael's idea, she intuited, of a woman swimming in drinking yoghurt was far too different to ever be approved by the client, let alone liked by the people it was talking to. As a piece of sales communication it failed. Now, if the woman was a cow, she thought, a cute cartoon cow that would only produce milk for the drinking yoghurt it loved so much…she paused, noticing that for the first time in a long time, her heart was beating fast.

The words came as quickly as the hours. It was midnight when she left the office and sunrise when she arrived back at her desk to retype her script, word perfect. When it was finished, a sense of calm enveloped her. She felt changed, as if some kind of shift had occurred within her. Her instincts were heightened, not in an excitable, adrenalin-fuelled way but in a way in which she saw very clearly what she must do, and when to do it.

The creative teams had gathered in the boardroom to present their ideas to Boss. After serving everyone drinks, she handed Boss her script. 'Here's another idea you might want to look at,' she said matter-of-factly. He looked at it, confused, 'Who wrote this?'

'I did,' she smiled, closing the door behind her.

BELIEVE

Believing is seeing. When you believe that your dreams can come true, your life will be a wonderful adventure filled with all you ever wanted. That's because what you believe – what you think – creates your future. Winston Churchill was right when he said 'You create your own universe as you go along.'

Many books have been written about this universal law of attraction as if it is some kind of secret, magical quality available only to a privileged few. What nonsense! The idea that your thoughts create your future is true for everyone, everywhere. You see it every day with everything you do.

The thought 'I'm hungry' leads you to find something to eat. The thought 'I want to catch the bus, not the train' creates an energy that enables you to catch the bus. How simple is that? It is so simple that we don't even think about it. But think about this: if you can change something so simple with your thoughts, you can change anything. Whatever you can imagine, you have the power to make it happen.

All you need to do is focus your energy and attention on what you want. If you don't focus on it, it won't happen. So, when you focus on catching the bus, you catch the bus. When you don't focus on catching the bus, you don't catch the bus. Change your thought, and you change your future.

It is the thought, the focus that you give to your dream that is the power that will make it come true. You can, of course, choose to keep your dream a dream. Millions of people have wishes and dreams but they don't give their dreams much thought, or they give up believing that their dream will ever come true. And so their dreams disappear, along with their hope for a happier future. Buddha illustrated this truth beautifully when he said, 'All that we are is a result of what we have thought.'

It is, though, natural to sometimes doubt that you can make your dream come true. But your doubts, as Shakespeare said, are your traitors. You need to trust that when you genuinely believe that you will succeed, you will. Of course you will make mistakes along the way. You may even fail, at first, in your mission. But what are failures but big mistakes? It is by making mistakes that you learn how to succeed. And if you never made a mistake, you would never learn.

Everyone makes mistakes. Even those whose talent or genius you might think comes naturally.

Vincent van Gogh knew only too well of the hard work and frustration that is so often a prelude to success when he said 'The thing has already taken form in my mind before I start it. The first attempts are absolutely unbearable. I say this, because I want you to know that if you see something worthwhile in what I am doing, it is not by accident but because of real direction and purpose.' Today, Van Gogh's paintings sell upwards of $100 million. Not bad for someone whose first attempts were 'unbearable.'

The biggest mistake you can make is to spend the rest of your life standing around worrying that you'll make a mistake. You have to jump in, make your mistakes, make your success, and make the life you dream of.

Because your thoughts create your future, it's important that you choose your thoughts carefully. Choosing your thoughts sounds simple enough, but it can be hard to practise.

We think about sixty thousand thoughts a day. Many of our thoughts, especially negative thoughts, have become ingrained in our minds and our minds have become quite attached to them. It takes awareness and some effort to change your negative thinking. If you find yourself thinking negatively, acknowledge that you are doing so and think, instead, about something or someone that makes you feel good. Keep that thought in your mind until you're no longer thinking negative thoughts. It can help to play music that makes you feel good, or look at a picture that you find uplifting.

The expression 'Be careful what you wish for' holds much truth. Because whatever you wish for, you can be sure that the Universe will give it to you. Be very clear about what you want. If you send out mixed messages you will get mixed results. Know what your dream is, write it down if it helps. Say it to yourself, or aloud, in the present tense, 'I am a travel journalist flying around the world.' 'I am living in a cottage by the sea.' 'I am driving a red convertible, I can smell the leather seats, I can feel the sun on my face.' Picture your dream in perfect detail. What does it look like and feel like? Does it have a sound? A scent? Who else is in the picture? If your dream involves an event, what time of day or night is it? What are you wearing? See it in all its detail and, more important, feel it as if it is occurring right now. Bring it into sharp focus, shape it and polish it until it shines like a light that illuminates your soul, and your entire being.

Above all, believe, believe, believe. If you don't believe, if you doubt that your dream will come true, than it won't. It's like buying something from a shop. You know you want a loaf of bread, so you go in and ask for it. You don't say 'I'd like some bread please, and I know you've got it but I don't think you'll give it to me.' No. Say 'I'd like some bread please,' and as you say it, see yourself taking it.

Because you must never let go of the belief that your dream will come true, it's important that you protect it from others. Do not talk about your dream to anyone who is not supportive. Keep it close to your heart, and guard it through difficult times. If it takes longer to materialise than you had hoped for and you start to feel fearful or full of doubt – which at times you surely will – shift your thought away from doubt to the positive belief that it will happen. Do not concern yourself yet with how it will happen, simply believe that it will happen.

Never underestimate the power of self-belief. Never – and this is possibly the most important bit – wish that it will happen one day. Believe it is happening now. Remember, the Universe is always keen to please, and never fails to give you more of what you focus on. Whatever you give your attention to becomes real. If you wish for something to happen in the future, the Universe will respond to the 'wishing it in the future' and in the future is where it will stay. The fact that you have already dreamed the dream and thought the thought means you are already bringing about the necessary changes. So, as difficult as it may be, believe that what you dream of is happening now, that you are now changing your life to become the person you want to be and you will see that, as sure as the moon rises and the sun sets, good things will begin to happen.

Writer and creator of classics including *Treasure Island*, Robert Louis Stevenson said 'To be what we are, and to become what we are capable of becoming, is the only end of life.' He understood that the real treasure in life is the treasure within you.

Inside you is pure potential just waiting to manifest. In this respect, you are no different from every living thing be it an ant or the Universe itself. It is whether or not you have spirit enough to reach into this deep well of potential and create something from it that will determine whether or not you manifest your dream. When you understand this simple yet profound concept, you don't simply believe, you know that anything is possible.

STRIVE

As the new junior copywriter, she worked the hardest and was paid the least. 'That's the way it should be,' her mother consoled her when she complained of her meagre salary, 'but it won't be that way forever.'

Forever was too far ahead to think about. All she could focus on was proving herself at the task at hand, and that required enormous effort and self-discipline. 'You're only as good as your next ad,' Boss growled at her. Yet his attitude towards her had softened since her 'cash cow' coup as it had become known. The commercial that she wrote had resulted in the most successful new product launch of the year, with sales nearly twice as high as predicted, and a bundle of new business for the agency.

Boss teamed her with Michael with whom she liked working and from whom she could learn a lot, especially when it came to the terrifying prospect of presenting her work. Michael's clean good looks, classic attire and striking blonde hair (made more charming by a natural quiff that refused to lie down) were matched by an easy self-assurance that comes from being happy with who you are. When he talked to clients, or anyone else for that matter, he spoke in a gentle manner, and treated them as if they were the only person in the room. She noticed that he always listened carefully to what others would say and he would never, not ever, argue with anyone. By being polite and charming and, above all, himself he deftly turned colleagues and clients around to his way of thinking. Whenever it came time for her to present her work and she felt her heart racing and her mouth turn dry, she thought of what Michael might say, and how he would say it. This way, she forgot her nerves and relaxed, and people listened to her.

When it came to writing, though, she worked alone, relying on her instincts to tell her when an idea was good enough, and when it was not. The more she trusted her instincts, the stronger they became. Of course there were times when she was consumed with self-doubt and afraid. Afraid that her bright idea was a one-off and that there were no more good ideas inside her. Afraid that she had inadvertently wandered into unfamiliar territory and that at any moment she would make a terrible mistake and a complete fool of herself. Afraid that the nagging discomfort she felt about her job was a warning she should perhaps heed. Afraid that, with no real friend to confide in, she might go mad with only herself to talk to. But mostly she was afraid that with each passing day, she was travelling further and further away from her dream. In spite of these fears, she was convinced that whatever it was that had taken hold of her that day and flooded her with inspiration was an opportunity and a gift, the likes of which she had never before experienced. Knowing this, she was aware that now was not the time to ask questions, now was the time to work.

And she worked. Day and night, night and day, she worked at her desk, in her bed, even when she was driving, wherever she could hold a pen. Weekends gave no respite as she laboured to meet deadlines, refine concepts and craft copy.

In spite of the soaring summer temperatures, she grew pale from staying indoors working. Some nights she did not sleep at all but would stay awake, pouring over advertising award annuals for inspiration, or gazing into the black night that turned more black before the dawn, and the pink, red and orange rays of the first sunlight that illuminated the room, informed her it was time to shower and leave for the agency.

On the occasions when she was spun dry with fatigue and no ideas would come, she would wander down to the harbour's edge and sit on a bench, listening to the clinking of the boats moored along the jetty, and the gentle, soothing sound of the water lapping by her feet. She would stare into the inky depths of the harbour and try to empty her mind. As she did so she found she could breathe more deeply, and with each newly refreshed breath came a spark of an idea that she could take away and mould into a commercial.

She had no time to play, only work. Having no social life was the price she paid for her demanding job. With no new news to report, her weekly conversations with her mother had become dull and repetitive. The weeks turned into months and then one day, the accolades and awards began to arrive.

'Is it real gold?' she stroked the Clio award on her desk.

'Gold plated,' Michael replied, not looking up from the storyboard he was drawing. She picked up the Clio award, it was heavy, a simple, striking figure, its arms held high above its head holding a stylised globe. Her hand wrapped around it, it felt smooth and cold, comfortable in her hand. She ran her fingers down its long, lean body, it was as beautiful to touch as it was to look at. She turned the figure around and as she did so, the sun caught it and cast golden rays of light into the room. The light was bright and so pure. She was enthralled. Was this light a reflection of her gift? Was this symbol of the ultimate advertising prize a symbol of her worth? Was this light that shone so clean and flooded her with a sense of excitement and anticipation and satisfaction the light that her mother had talked about? Was this the light she must follow?

Watching the light dance around the room, she knew that she had achieved something important. It was an intoxicating feeling. She felt the heavy weight of the statue in her hand and smiled at the thought that she was worth her weight in gold. She turned it again, and again it cast its magic rays of light around the pink walls and the pictures of her work. 'I think it's real gold,' she said. Michael looked up from his work and smiled, he knew how hard she had worked, and he recognised her talent. 'Maybe. Give it here,' he reached across to take it. And as he did so, the light caught his blonde hair and for a moment, she thought, he looked like an angel.

That evening she didn't go straight home after work. Instead, she walked down to the waterfront at Blues Point and sat and looked across the water at the city skyscrapers stretching into the darkening sky. For a long time she sat thinking of little else but her award, her prize for all her efforts, and she luxuriated in the feeling of satisfaction that it brought. And though she felt entitled to enjoy her reward, she knew full well that the hard work had only just begun. If anything, more was now demanded of her and the challenge to always beat her previous best was a hard one. Suddenly she felt tired, and wanted her bed. When she opened the door to her home, there was an envelope on the doormat. It was an early birthday card from her mother, a reminder of the date, and the fact that her visa was about to expire and, with it, her newfound success.

STRIVE

What is it that you must do to make your dream come true? Do you need to make a phone call? Read a book? Sign up for a course? Apply for a job? Visit someone or some place? If you know what you need to do, what are you waiting for? Tomorrow? If you're waiting for tomorrow, know that tomorrow never comes. All that matters is this day, and what you do with it.

Whatever it is you want to achieve, you have to start now. Successful people approach everything they do with a sense of urgency. They don't put things off, and they don't waste time procrastinating. Successful people don't talk the talk, they walk the walk. Nor do they attribute their success to good luck. Successful people make their own luck. They know that luck is nothing more than being prepared and trusting in the outcome.

If you have built castles in the air, now you need to build the foundations. An idea on its own cannot change a thing, you must apply effort in the right direction. As well as effort, it takes courage to do the thing you think you cannot. But you must find the courage because if you don't, you will spend the rest of your life wondering what you could have done, and who you could have been. The Chinese philosopher, Lao-Tzu said 'The journey of a thousand miles begins with a single step.' So take that step, pick up the phone, call that contact, knock on that door, arrange that meeting, make the move. Stop thinking about it, and do it. Soon, the doing will take over and you will be on your way to living the life you are meant to live.

Sometimes we have obligations to others that stop us from immediately following our dreams. It is important that you fulfil these obligations, knowing that once you've done so, you will feel lighter and will be free to pursue your passion. If you find yourself temporarily bound to a situation that demands your time and attention, do not begrudge it, but focus on what you have to do with care and attention, so that you can get through it and move on.

It's also important to understand that your purpose in life, your dharma, is not necessarily your job. It's wonderful if you can make your passion your career, but it may be something you do in your spare time, be it teaching football, planting a forest or learning a new language. In his book *Manual of the Warrior of Light*, Paulo Coelho describes how his warrior sometimes feels as if he were living two lives at once; one life of obligation, doing things in which he does not believe, and another life filled with dreams. At a certain point, the two lives become one: 'There is a bridge that links what I do with what I would like to do,' he thinks. Slowly, his dreams take over his everyday life, and then he realises that he is ready for the thing he always wanted. Then all that is needed is a little daring, and his two lives become one.'

Do not be afraid to try new things. Fortune, remember, favours the bold.

Your soul can only grow through change. If you are faced with a choice and need to decide which path to take, ask yourself which is the more limiting decision? Which path forces you to dismiss any new or different ideas? Do not choose the path that limits you in this way. It will strangle your life, and your future. Choose the path that, instead of narrowing future possibilities, expands your ideas. If you start to feel uncomfortable with your choice, it is a warning that you are making the wrong decision.

When you choose the uncertain, you are choosing something that will make you feel alive. It can be both the best and the worst of feelings. The exhilaration in your soul may at times be drowned out by screaming voices within you – and around you, voices that yell at you to stop, go back, do not attempt to sail into uncharted waters. But know that, though your voyage will not always be smooth and you will encounter obstacles, setbacks and rejections along the way, you must accept the challenge to turn your dream into reality.

If you make a mistake, as you surely will, if you take a wrong turn, if you fall off the horse, stand up, brush yourself down and get back on. Failure is not the falling down, it's the staying down. Do not quit. No-one ever made their dreams come true by quitting. Change course if necessary, take a different path if it's better, but do not change your dream. The teacher of ancient wisdom, Torkom Saraydarian wrote 'Changing your goal often is like changing the location of your tree. It will eventually dry up.' Understanding that failure is frequently a precursor to success, he also wrote 'The Soul does not approve of failure; it challenges the human being again and again until he overcomes his weaknesses.'

Sometimes, though, progress can be measured more by your setbacks than successes. This is certainly true of the story of one famous American who, like millions of others, took up the challenge to make his dreams come true. In 1832, after failing in business, he ran for a seat in Illinois State Legislature, and lost. The next year, he ran again and, again, lost. In 1835, his girlfriend died and he suffered a nervous breakdown. He fought back from ill health and, five years later, he ran for State Elector. In 1843 he ran for Congress, and was defeated. He was defeated again in 1848. In 1855 he ran for the Senate and was defeated. He was again defeated in 1856 when he ran for Vice Presidency of the United States. In 1858 he ran for the Senate again, and he lost. Did this man ever stop trying? Did he ever give up? No. His name was Abraham Lincoln, and in 1869, some 38 years after his business failed, he was elected President of the United States of America.

The bigger your dream and the more steps you have to take to reach it, the bigger your reward. There will be times when you find the enormity of your task overwhelming, and you question why you have chosen this mission, and how you can possibly see it through. It is natural to feel this way. Understand that you are never given more than you can cope with, and when it all becomes too hard, too daunting, consider this: you can eat an elephant. How? You take one bite at a time.

Concentrate only on the task immediately in

front of you, and you will complete it. Then, and only then, think about the next task. This is how you climb the mountain, slowly, one step at a time. This is how you reach the top. And remember, the higher the mountain, the more beautiful the view from the top.

Don't even think about whether or not you will succeed, nor worry about how you will succeed. Think, instead, of the many ways in which you will. It will help you to know that you can concentrate better, and produce better results when you are absorbed, mind, body and soul, in the task. It takes a little skill and a lot of practice to achieve the concentration necessary to sustain you through prolonged periods of hard work. Real concentration is when you become totally immersed in whatever you are doing. It's when you become so completely engaged, that wandering thoughts cannot take over and distractions disappear. By practising being 'in the moment' you can sharpen your focus, develop better judgement and achieve greater success in less time, and with less apparent effort.

Start practising by becoming absorbed in simple everyday tasks – to the exclusion of all other thoughts. Next time you are washing yourself, try not to think about anything else, but focus on every aspect of what you are doing. What does the soap feel and smell like? What sound does the water make? How does it feel on your skin? Concentrate on each part of your body as you wash. When you practise becoming focussed and present in this way, you discover that each and every job you do, from the mundane to the meaningful, is done with awareness, precision and skill.

When you strive to fulfil your purpose in life, when you work hard to make your dream come true, you will find help and inspiration comes to you, often from the least expected places. You will also find, paradoxically, amidst the late nights, early starts, deadlines and extreme effort, a growing sense of inner calm and peace, the peace that comes from knowing that you are living your truth, and living your life.

TRUST

On the same day that she and Michael moved into an office with a panoramic harbour view, Boss informed her that her salary would be doubled. Overnight. And, for the first time since she had arrived, she joined her colleagues for lunch at an expensive restaurant where many advertising people dined and drank and where Boss drank the most. 'Here she is, the golden girl,' a fellow copywriter held his arms out, welcoming her to their table, 'What are you drinking, pet?' It felt good to be recognised as one of the team, to be part of the friendly banter, the jibing and joking. She'd never before associated work with fun, at least not the kind of fun where you're encouraged to get drunk. She enjoyed the way the wine relaxed her and made it easy to talk to those she had once been in awe of. She liked feeling the tension drain out of her, and the sense of lightness that enabled her to laugh at others and herself. Even Michael, who was usually very conscious of not allowing any kind of pleasure interfere with his work, appeared relaxed and carefree as the bottles kept coming, and the afternoon escaped into the night.

Money can buy you nice lunches. It can buy you beautiful clothes and belongings. And money can buy you time…in the form of a husband, and a resident's visa.

Michael's friend, Billy, lived in a small boathouse on the edge of Pittwater, a calm and sheltered waterway protected by a richly forested peninsular, the other side of which raged the Pacific Ocean. Though it may once have housed a boat, the building was now little more than a large, crumbling shed that could only be accessed by water or – as she and Michael had arrived – by descending 101 steep, slippery steps that zigzagged their way down to the water from a dirt track above.

The boathouse consisted of just one room with a raised sleeping platform, and an outdoor shower and toilet that was constructed of rocks and stones and was full of holes, and which reminded her of a scene from *The Flintstones*. Along the entire length of the building, facing the water were floor to ceiling windows with a sliding glass door that opened onto a rickety balcony that also ran the length of the building.

It was late afternoon when she and Michael arrived and were ushered onto the balcony and a creaking old wicker sofa, while Billy made them mugs of tea. The winter sun lay low on the horizon, and with the water lapping a few feet below, the early evening call of kookaburras pierced the otherwise quiet air. Jem looked across the narrow stretch of water to the forest of eucalyptus trees interspersed with honey coloured sandstone rocks, and was utterly entranced. Away from all that was wrong with the world, and close to all that mattered, she felt an almost extra sensory vibration in the air, as if every moment was heavy with meaning or, if it wasn't, it should be.

'Woah…there goes dinner,' laughed Billy as he returned to rescue the fishing line that was straining over the balcony. The water below splashed with the one that got away. She watched him as he reeled in the line and observed that he looked quite the regular Aussie bushman in his khaki shorts, t-shirt and battered old Squatter's hat. He was tall and slender, bordering on thin, but nonetheless good looking in an earthy Australian kind of way. His brown sun-kissed hair was long and unkempt, rather like his whole appearance which was slightly crumpled. She noticed a scar on his tanned forehead. 'Caught a couple of Kingfish this arvo, you can even get Dory this time o' year,' Billy skilfully reset his line, 'if you're lucky,' he added. His copper coloured cattle dog, Red, looked up at him expectantly and sighed as it slumped its head against the timber boards, its ears twitching to keep away the flies.

Jem leaned back on the creaking sofa, and breathed in the clean air, 'I never want to leave,' she said, turning her face to the setting sun and closing her eyes, and the two men laughed.

Maybe it was the heat. Maybe it was the water. Maybe it was the magic. Whatever it was, a sleepy peacefulness hung over the trio. Time slows down when you're next to nature. There's a stillness and a serenity that seeps into every moment and every thing. Events happen in slow motion and even the simple ritual of making tea becomes a significant production. Billy handed her a chipped mug and she noticed his bony hands, weathered from the sun.

He explained that he needed the money for repairs to his home. For reasons she thought best not to enquire about, he didn't have a job. The large sum of money she was offering in return for a marriage certificate would go a long way, she could see that. She didn't begrudge him his fee. He was, after all, going to earn it and she was grateful for that. More than grateful, she was relieved. Relieved that she, or rather Michael, knew someone willing to undertake such a huge commitment, to go through a marriage ceremony, to lie to the authorities in order to help her stay in Australia and forge her career. Billy was perfect. He was of a similar age to her, he was intelligent and he had the wherewithal to handle the inevitable questioning they would face in her application for residency. He was also, she quickly deduced, a good person. She liked him and given the precarious situation she was now in, that was a real bonus.

'You know he's gay,' Michael said, as he drove her home.

'Is he?' she feigned surprise. She had thought as much but had learned not to assume anything anymore.

'He won't hurt you, Billy wouldn't hurt anyone,' Michael continued, sensing her insecurity.

'Just so long as he turns up on the day,' was all she said.

She had bought a husband and made a friend. The wedding took place on a grey Saturday afternoon in a small, windowless room on the 13th floor of the New South Wales Registry of Births, Deaths and Marriages in Sydney's Civic Centre. Witnesses to the ceremony and the only guests present were Michael and a beautiful young Chinese woman he introduced as Sunny. Afterwards, they walked across George Street to The Regent Hotel where, in the plush comfort of The Piano Bar, they drank cocktails in celebration of the event.

They laughed as they took photos, she and Billy posing as a bride and groom would pose with Michael, the best man looking on, smiling his approval. Now that the deed was done, she felt lighter. She refused to dwell on the illegality of the reason for the marriage because although she lived by society's rules, she had never needed an authority to tell her who she was, and what she could do. If she was doing no harm, she believed, it was no problem. At this moment, she basked in the relief that fate had dealt her a trump card that she had played well to secure her future. Was it the same future she had dreamed of when she arrived a year ago? When she asked herself that question, she couldn't answer, and this uncertainty sent shivers of apprehension through her. A year ago she knew exactly what she wanted and where she was going. Now, unsure of the direction in which she was travelling, there was a gnawing sensation that her life had been blown off course, and she had become lost, stranded in a place very different to where she wanted to be.

She looked at the ring on her finger, the one that she and Billy had bought yesterday in the Dollar Days shop. It was silver coloured plastic with a blue heart shaped gem, cut to look like a real jewel. They had fun choosing it, 'Only the best for the best,' laughed Billy as he went down on one knee and slipped it on her finger. Now, as she looked at it, she felt slightly sick, the confidence she felt just moments before was obliterated by a deep sense of insecurity, and waves of panic. The blue plastic heart was a stark symbol of all that was fake in her life – the husband, the marriage, the dream. In the back of her mind a voice was screaming at her to stop, like the warning sign you see on the city freeway written in big black letters that reads: WRONG WAY – GO BACK. But which way was back? Back home to her mother with whom her weekly phone calls had now dwindled to once a month and who knew nothing of her visa problem, or solution. No, she couldn't go back. And if she no longer knew which way was forward, then all she could do was trust in the present.

She looked around at the genteel crowd that mingled under the glittering chandeliers, and at her friends who were ordering more cocktails. 'I'll have another Golden Dream,' she said laughing, a little too loudly, at the drinks waiter standing patiently at their table.

TRUST

Once you are clear about what it is you want, and you are consciously striving towards your goal, there is little more you can do except trust that your dream will come true. There will no doubt be times when the world seems to be conspiring against you, and you feel that the wind is blowing your life – and your dream – off course. But any setbacks or shifts in direction are not to be interpreted as a sign of failure. Trust that your vision will materialise, trust and let it go. If you cling too tightly to a fixed idea of exactly how and when it will materialise, you are not allowing the creative energy of the Universe do its work. And there is nothing more creative than the Universe, or more capable of manifesting your desires.

Look around at nature and you can see evidence of how the Universe works in perfect synchronicity. The seasons come and go on time, the birds find food to eat, the sun ripens the corn. If you trust the Universe to manage nature so harmoniously, trust too that it will deliver your goals. But if you cling to a fixed outcome, it's as if you doubt nature's intelligence and its power to organise everything just the way it should.

Many people are now writing about the concept of wish-practice. They are careful to highlight the importance of letting go of total control and getting 'out of the way' to enable other energies to enter and help make your wish come true. You can't force your wish (or anything else for that matter) to manifest. On the contrary, it appears that wishes seem to come true the moment you look away. If you are constantly obsessing about your wish, you are not giving it the space it needs to work its magic.

Trust, and let go of any rigid thinking you have. Be receptive to new opportunities that will come towards you. This means you need to detach from trying to solve all the problems and answer all the questions in front of you. It does not mean that you detach or let go of your goal. Nor does it mean you stop working towards it. It simply means that you stop worrying about how it will fall into place. The moment you stop worrying about how and when it will work is the moment you see evidence that it's working. When you are willing to let go of any rigid thinking, you create the space for spontaneous answers to appear naturally. That's the beauty, the creativity of the Universe at work.

'Don't worry, be happy' is an expression that

we all know. It originated from the Indian spiritual thinker Sri Bhagwan Rajneesh. But few people know that what Bhagwan Rajneesh actually said was 'Do your best, then don't worry, be happy.' He knew, like all teachers of wisdom know, that if you do your best, the Universe will do the rest.

There are times, of course, when we need to worry. As humans, we are physiologically wired to worry in order to survive. Sometimes, we need to spring into action because of a real and immediate threat, and worry is the mechanism that forces us to take action. The rest of the time, worrying is useless. It doesn't take you anywhere, it only takes up valuable thinking time that could be better spent on something else. The word worry comes from the old English word 'wyrgan' which means to strangle. And that's what worrying does, it strangles the life and creativity out of all other thoughts and energy. On a physical level, worry creates anxiety, paralysis and depression.

So, if you're worried by what the future holds, stop. Remember the words in The Beatles song, 'Let it be.' You have announced your future and are striving to secure it. Learn to go with the flow and not say 'no' to any idea that helps you, even if it means you have to take a different approach from the one you planned. There is more than one path up the mountain, and it might be the path that you cannot see at first that leads you on a better journey, and to a better place.

Say, for example, you're finding it difficult to find work as a singer when out of the blue you're offered acting work in a stage musical. Do you turn it down? Perhaps you would be wise to grasp the opportunity, jump into the uncertainty of the role in the awareness that it might help your goal of being a singer, and may even turn out to be more exciting.

What if you wish to live in a house with a stream at the bottom of the garden and instead you find a house with a garden that has a wildlife pond? Will you say 'no'? Maybe there's a good reason why it's better not to have a stream. Maybe the house won't flood in heavy rain.

It's important that, as with any goal you have, you stay focussed on your dream but are flexible in how you achieve it. The Universe will reveal its plan for you; you simply have to be open to receive it. If you understand that your thoughts always turn into events or things in your life, and that all you have to do is allow yourself to flow with your dream, then that will is enough.

To trust means to accept the situation – every

situation – for what it is, and not try to pit yourself against the force of the Universe. Focus on what's taking place in the present moment, move with it, and the future will take care of itself. Look upon every difficulty or problem as an opportunity to be explored, and you will find yourself in the flow of nature and on the road to making your dreams come true. Of that, you can trust.

PROSPER

In Australian Vogue it says that you should never wear anything you don't love, really love, and that the only way to buy clothes you love is to try them on without looking at the price tag. Old habits though are hard to break, and the notion of giving up shopping for clothes in the city's downtown factory outlets was proving more difficult than she imagined. Until she spotted the dress.

It was the colour of burnished gold. Tightly fitted across the chest, it fell in gentle swathes from the waist, reminiscent of the style worn by a Grecian goddess. Around the neckline and decorating the waistband were sparkling stones of amber, topaz and citrine, so the overall effect when she moved was of shimmering sands. It cost a week's wages, but she didn't yet realise that, having dutifully followed the magazine's advice and tried it on without looking at the price tag.

They say that money can't buy you happiness but as she unwrapped the dress at home, carefully peeling back the layers of fine tissue paper, and as she held it up against herself in the mirror, she couldn't remember the last time she had felt so happy. Any guilt she felt over its price was quickly banished with the thought that next month would bring another large pay cheque and, if she desired, another designer dress.

At twenty-three, she was earning more money than she could have dreamed of. And spending more than she thought possible. Yet along with her increasing wealth came a corresponding lack of time, time to rest, time to play, time to dream or at least remember the dream she once had. She wanted to move to a nicer apartment or even a little weatherboard house overlooking the water. But she never had enough time to look for anywhere else. She never had enough time to do anything except work, and although the leap in salary was welcome, it came at a price. The constant challenge to create something out of nothing was exciting but it was also exhausting, and the sense of achievement she felt was always short lived – as short as the time as it took for the next brief to land on her desk, and another late night of mind-bending, gut-wrenching, nail-biting labour to give birth to a new campaign.

The more she worked, the more she was valued, the more she earned, the more she worked. If she was feeling tired, she told herself that it was a good tired, the kind of tired that is the result of hard work. But each night, she found it more and more difficult to get to sleep and when she finally did, she dreamed the same dream; she was clinging onto the roof of a speeding train hurtling past all the stations, never stopping. On and on it went, faster and faster, she wanted to get off but she knew that if she jumped, she would be killed. So she clung to the roof, narrowly avoiding being decapitated as the train tore through dark tunnels, waiting, wishing, willing for the train to stop.

Billy whistled his approval, and she laughed as she twirled coquettishly, the jewels on the dress sparkling under the light of the moon. 'Champagne's on ice and you're hot!' She cringed at his embarrassing attempt at a compliment, and laughed in delight as he reeled in a fishing line from the water at the end of which was tied a bottle of Moet. Billy had exchanged his everyday shorts and t-shirt for a dark blue suit that, despite being too big for his slender frame, made him look extraordinarily handsome. 'And you look perfect,' she replied, 'we've got to be there in an hour.'

'Well, we better drink up then.' He handed her a glass of champagne, and she stifled a yawn as they raised glasses.

'You're not going to leave the party early again, are you?' Billy peered at her over the rim of his glass.

'Sorry, it's been a big week.'

'And it's going to be a big night – your night. You want to make the most of it.' He moved to the bench top in the kitchen area where, neatly laid out on a breadboard, were lines of cocaine. 'Ladies first,' he smiled, handing her a ready-rolled ten dollar note. Why not? she thought. It could do no harm.

The next day she woke up late, her head hot and sore, her mouth dry. The unforgiving sunlight poured though the window and she turned away from its glare, scanning her memory, trying to recall the events of the night before.

She remembered arriving with Billy for the awards ceremony at the Art Gallery of New South Wales, and looking up at the elegant neoclassical building illuminated against the night sky and dark trees. She remembered feeling like a princess as Billy took her hand and she stepped out of the cab in her dazzling dress.

She remembered meeting Michael, and sitting next to Sunny who, dressed in a traditional cheongsam the colour of sapphires, looked like a porcelain doll. She relived the moment that she was struck by Sunny's beauty, her gentle, kind brown eyes, flawless skin and her lips which were unusually large, the kind of lips that men want to kiss. She remembered Billy remarking that Sunny's real name was Sun Ye, but everyone had always called her Sunny. It was not hard to see why. Sunny had the sweetest, most graceful disposition with a smile that could span Sydney Harbour. Next to Sunny, Jem (whose body was perfectly contoured) felt large and distinctly unfeminine. She recalled how Sunny looked at Michael with complete adoration, and how he took her tiny hand in his and kissed it. She remembered how she had felt a sudden stab of jealousy and how, taken aback by the force of her emotion, she had immediately dismissed the feeling as an effect of the drink and drugs. Sunny has goodness in her heart, she had told herself, and they are made for each other.

Her melancholy quickly turned to jubilation when hers and Michael's commercial for Coca-Cola was announced as best television commercial of the year. She leapt up in excitement and, with Michael behind her, almost ran up to the stage to collect their award, and she remembered – how could she forget

– walking back to the agency table and seeing Boss clapping enthusiastically, a fat cigar in his mouth which, when he stood up to congratulate her, fell into his glass of champagne. She remembered that the room got darker and louder and she started to feel sick and she walked, no, ran out of the room asking a security guard for directions to the toilet. He led her to a lift that was covered, floor to ceiling, in blue carpet and she remembered that her mind – which seemed have gone into overdrive and was incapable of slowing down – had deduced that the carpet was there to protect the gallery's paintings. She remembered that the guard waited for her outside the ladies and she groaned when she remembered that he must have heard her vomiting. He escorted her back to the ballroom where there was more champagne and laughter.

She remembered clearly thinking (does cocaine make you think more clearly or do you just think you think more clearly?) but she remembered a very lucid moment when she seemed to step outside herself and she saw herself drinking and smoking which was strange because she never smoked, and thinking that it wasn't her at all but an impostor. After that, she remembered nothing. The phone rang and she reached across the bed to answer it, it was

Billy. 'Champagne gives you the worst hangovers, you know,' he said.

She lay back on her pillow, nursing her forehead in her hands and looked at her clothes strewn across the room; her new shoes scuffed and dirty, her dress lying crumpled on the floor. Some threads had come loose and had started to unravel. Like the threads of my dream, she thought, unravelling before me. And as hard as she tried, she couldn't think of a way to gather them up and sew them back together again.

PROSPER

In what wonderful ways do you blossom and grow? Where in your life or in your Self are you blessed with abundance? And where can you benefit from even greater prosperity?

When we hear the word 'prosper', we automatically think of it in terms of money because in today's world money is how most people measure success. Yet there are many forms of prosperity of which money is probably the least important. How can you be sure of this? Think, for a moment, of all that you have that money cannot buy. Do you have friends? A loving family? A clever mind? A rich imagination? Are you healthy? If you are blessed with any of these gifts, then you are prosperous in ways that are infinitely more valuable than money. Now, imagine if you were able to replace what you have with more money. Would you sacrifice your health or that of your loved ones for a few more dollars? Would you want to be rich if it meant you were lonely? Financial prosperity is worth less without physical, emotional and spiritual prosperity, and the old cliché 'money can't buy happiness' rings true for everyone.

Yet in our consumer-driven society, most everywhere we go we are told to get more, have more, buy more. And we blindly follow this instruction without questioning where – or who – it's coming from, and whether or not it is the right thing to do. We run ourselves ragged earning money just to spend it, and spending it so that we have to earn it, often spending it before we earn it. We compare ourselves to others and we are tricked into believing that if we have what others have, we will be happy. But it is a lie and deep down we know it. We sense that acquiring material things – expensive cars, designer clothes and grand houses – does little or nothing to make us truly happy. If it did, why would we keep wanting more?

Of course, there are material things that you need to have to live happily. 'We're living in a material world, and I am a material girl,' sang Madonna in her 1985 signature song. You need a decent place to live as your environment has a huge effect on how you feel. You need to eat good food to stay healthy. You need a good car, it is your workhorse and it has to work efficiently. You need to wear nice clothes because, like it or not, your appearance is important. Coco Chanel was right when she said 'Dress shabbily and they remember the dress; dress impeccably and they remember the woman.'

Not only do you need these things for your wellbeing but you deserve them, too. In fact, there is no-one more deserving of all the bounty that the Universe has to offer than you. If you find that hard to believe, ask yourself why the person standing next to you deserves more and you'll be unable to come up with a good answer. You are no less – or more – deserving than anyone else, and if you believe yourself to be worth less, think again. Success isn't reserved for an elite few, it's something everyone is capable of achieving. You are just as entitled to your share of good things, so long as you acquire it through wise action.

Anyone who has lived on Struggle Street will appreciate that having money makes life a lot easier. If you want to attract more money into your life and become financially prosperous, there are ways you can do this.

First, think about all those ways in which you are already rich and prosperous, really think about them and as you do so, give thanks for them. Perhaps you are blessed with a healthy child, an abundance of creativity, a loyal friend or a loving partner. Maybe you can be thankful for the small pleasures – a beautiful rose in your garden, a freshly brewed cup of coffee, a new book by your favourite author. Whatever it is, counting your blessings; expressing genuine heartfelt thankfulness for what you have is one of the most powerful things you can do. Research shows that people who are grateful are generally happier, more energetic and less materialistic.

When you appreciate and give thanks for what you have instead of focussing on what you don't have – your thoughts will return you more. The Universe always gives you more of what you focus on because your thoughts contain a very real energy. Remember to express your gratitude in the present tense. Do not ask for what you want to happen in the future, but give thanks for the fact that you already have it. The energy then expands on the 'having it' as opposed to the 'wanting it'.

A simple way to express gratitude for what you have (and thereby attract more) is to say aloud, or silently 'I give thanks for …' whatever it is you are thankful for. For example, say 'I give thanks for my good health,' and you will notice that simply by focussing on your good health, you become healthier. It takes a little practice and repetition. Keep on giving thanks for your good health for a few minutes every day, and you will find yourself quite naturally taking steps to stay healthy. What's more, the Universe will send you help, often in unexpected ways.

This simple but powerful practice can be applied to anything you want to acquire more of, including money. Get into the habit of saying something like 'I give thanks for the income that flows into my life that enables me to pay my bills completely and on time.' Or, 'I give thanks for the financial success that is now coming to me.' Choose your words carefully. Whatever it is you want, be clear, be specific, and be assured it is coming to you right now.

Prosperity thinking is nothing new, it's as ancient as the hills, and when you practise it with a genuine commitment, it works. Whatever it is that you have that you want more of, by saying thank you for it with sincere appreciation and gratitude, you will attract more, much more.

Of course, the opposite is true. When you talk about lack of money (or any other thing for that matter) you are affirming poverty, and bringing more of the same into your life. Keep telling yourself and others that you are 'broke' and can't afford to pay the bills, and you will continue to prove yourself right. Next time you find yourself moaning about the cost of living to a friend, or complaining about how expensive things are, stop before you speak the words (or better still, before you think the thought). If you indulge in poverty thinking, you will make your words come true. Whatever it is you want more of, focus on it and give thanks for it because the truth is that it already exists. There is plenty to go around, and unlimited potential for you to access. You are the creator of your own prosperity and there is nothing you cannot have if you are prepared to grasp the opportunities that come your way. You can make your prosperity bigger or smaller depending on the thoughts you choose to think. Money, friendships, love – the only person who might prevent abundance coming to you, is you.

Sometimes, when you are lacking, the divide between the have's and the have not's seems especially cruel and unfair. At times like this, do not put yourself in the 'have not' camp by focussing on your lack. Nor begrudge others their success and happiness. Instead, be pleased for them, and know that their good fortune is also your good fortune, and the more genuinely happy you are for their prosperity, the more prosperous you will become. When you resent others people's success, you limit your own. How it can it be otherwise? After all, consciousness is infinite, and therefore there is always enough. When we choose to denigrate someone else's prosperity, we prevent that infinite flow of abundance reaching us.

When we appreciate that money is a commodity, an object that is no more or less physical than the water in the river, or the leaves on the trees, we can see that it operates by the same laws. When it's full up, there is no room for more. You cannot pour more water into a lake that is already full. You cannot add more money into a bank account that is full enough to meet your needs. Only when the lake begins to empty is there space for more water to come in. And only when you don't have the money you need are you able to attract more. This means that you need to keep your money circulating. Your money needs to go out in order to flow back in again, and that means you have to spend your money wisely, or give it away to create the space into which more can return. The lyrics of the children's song *The Magic Penny* echo this truth:

Love is something if you give it away,
give it away, give it away.
Love is something if you give it away,
you end up having more.

It's just like a magic penny,
hold it tight and you won't have any.
Lend it, spend and you'll have so many,
they'll roll all over the floor.

Miserliness is such an unattractive trait. Have you ever noticed how some very wealthy people are reluctant to spend their money or give it away? And how it is so often the people who have less money who are more generous? If they appear happier than those who 'hold their money tight' it is because they are happier. They have learned the truth that 'it's better to give than to receive'. They know that when you give – and give joyfully – what you get in return is worth much more. They also appreciate what some very wealthy people don't – that when you give, you don't spiral downwards into a black hole from which you will never escape. On the contrary, you vacate space for what you give – and more – to return. In all the literature on happiness, one commonly held belief is that being kind to others can trigger an avalanche of positive consequences.

It's important that when you give, you give from your heart. If, when you give, you think 'I'm always shelling out,' or 'Why is it always me who has to cough up?' you are begrudging what you give and need to change your attitude. Next time you feel put upon, ask yourself if you would feel happier giving if you knew that more would be sure to flow back in. When you give from your heart – be it money, love, time or effort – you always get more back.

It takes faith to give your money away, especially if you don't have much to give. In ancient times tithing, as it is called, was common practice. The individual voluntarily 'tithed' one-tenth of his or her income to support the spiritual organisation that, in turn, supported the community. Whether or not you agree with the principle of tithing, it represents a timeless and universal law; whenever you give unconditionally and from the heart, your prosperity will increase dramatically. When you are willing to give what it is you want, you keep the abundance of the Universe flowing.

But what if you simply have no money to give? In that case, give something you do have, donate your services, your skill, give your appreciation in the form of a thank you note, give a compliment, or a smile. Or give what is perhaps the most precious gift of all, your time. Volunteer to help at your local school, visit someone who is lonely, cook a meal for someone, or help do something for the community.

Whatever you choose to give, give it gladly and you will not only discover your gift is returned, you will also discover a deep feeling of joy that is the real reward of giving.

Far from being just an old fashioned notion, the joy derived from giving has a solid scientific basis. In the medical study *Inner Workings of the Magnanimous Mind* by the National Institute of Neurological Disorders and Strokes, it was discovered that the act of giving or making a donation heightened activity in parts of the midbrain, a region connected to primal desires such as food and sex. Dr Jorge Moll, the neurologist who led the research, said 'Many people think they should not do anything for others unless it has a material benefit for themselves but our brains show you profit emotionally from doing so. Something in our brain is shaped by evolution which allows us to feel joy when we do good things.'

There are some people who take what they think is a spiritual approach to money to the extreme. In their search for a more meaningful existence they choose to turn their back on the material world altogether. They believe there is something wrong in having plenty of money, and that you cannot be both spiritually and financially prosperous. But their thinking is misguided. The French writer, Albert Camus wrote, 'It is a kind of spiritual snobbery that makes people think they can be happy without money.'

Being poor is not the pathway to enlightenment. It's nonsense to think that you have to be poor to be spiritual. Only if your money is earned by hurting other people or manipulating them in some way (and there are many ways in which you can manipulate others) is it wrong. Likewise, if you take what doesn't belong to you, you will lose it. If you lie, steal or cheat someone out of what is rightfully theirs, you will lose what you take, and more. Remember, cheats never prosper. If, on the other hand, your money is earned by helping or serving others, if your prosperity is a result of honest and good business practice, then your money and wealth is a blessing and one you can enjoy to the fullest.

The same principle can be applied to the people who work for you, and with you. Showing respect to your employees guarantees they will respect you in return. Every successful entrepreneur knows that you don't have to be a ruthless back-stabber to succeed. Martha Lane Fox, co-founder of Lastminute.com made her first million before she was 30, and then floated the company for

£571 million. She founded her business on sound humanitarian principles, saying 'I strongly believe you don't have to be a horrible person to own your own company. Yes, business can be tough but you can make friends along the way.'

Work for the benefit of others, yes, and give what you can but most important, give to yourself. Above all, give yourself time. Do not allow making money to become your primary focus. If you do, your money will eat you up, and you will be lost. Author and motivational speaker, Wayne Dwyer spoke of how his wealth increased dramatically when he stopped focussing on making money, 'When I chased money, I never had enough. When I got my life on purpose and focussed on giving of myself and everything that arrived into my life, then I was prosperous.'

If you seek financial security you can chase it for a lifetime and never find it, because security can never come from material wealth alone. People say 'When I have a million dollars, then I'll be financially secure.' But it never happens. Becoming attached to money and security only creates insecurity, no matter how much money you have in the bank. How many times do you hear stories of people whose lives or relationships have fallen apart because the desire to earn money has overtaken the importance of more lasting, meaningful blessings in their life? How many people grow old and realise, too late, that you can always make more money, but you cannot make more time. American philosopher, Ralph Waldo Emerson summed it up when he said 'Money often costs too much.'

Strive to prosper, make your money, enjoy your home, your beautiful clothes and belongings, but not at the expense of your health, your family, or your Self.

True prosperity is having much more than money. True prosperity is a way of thinking, living and being. It is acknowledging and being truly grateful for the blessings in your life; a child's laughter, a warm kitchen filled with delicious smells of cooking, sunshine on your face, rain on your garden, gladness in your heart. True prosperity is the feeling of peace and contentment that comes with knowing that you have all that you want, and want all that you have. This is true prosperity. And no amount of money can buy it.

BALANCE

Her life assumed a pattern, of sorts. The days tumbled into weeks and summer passed quickly. The demands of her job, though, did not abate. The pressure on her to perform was relentless and was relieved only by evenings spent relaxing over drinks with colleagues at the local wine bar, The Grape Escape, and weekends spent with Billy whose friendship had become a comfort and whose home had become a retreat; a place where each step down to the water's edge was a step further away from the outside world, a place where there was no pressure and she felt safe.

Over many days and evenings they spent together drinking beer on the balcony overlooking the silent water, she learned that Billy, like Michael, was an art director, only Billy was 'more the art and less the director,' he said, pointing to a bundle of painted canvases stacked neatly in the corner of the boathouse. 'Hated it, hated the people, the work, the bloody clients, not like Michael – he was born for the job.' Billy took a long drink from his can of beer. He went on to describe how they had first met at art college in Sydney, Michael, a local boy, and Billy, a 'Bushie' from 'Woop Woop'. She looked incredulous. 'Mungerannie. The outback,' he explained, 'Beyond the black stump, middle of bloody nowhere. Nearest town, Birdsville, 300k's away, one pub and a handful of houses. Nearest airport, Broken Hill, two days drive away, full of miners and prostitutes,' he paused, 'and artists.' He was quiet for a moment, lost somewhere back in the place he had years ago chosen to leave. His parents, he said, managed to scratch out a living running a roadhouse in the middle of the Sturt Stony Desert, 'a place people run away to when they don't want to be found,' he said, 'and where the only visitors are stockmen stopping to refuel and truckies who need a bunk for the night. Oh, and the occasional taipan, the most poisonous snake in the world,' he said, grinning.

She thought there could be no place on earth more different to London. 'We're the same, you and me,' she said placing her hand on top of his in a gesture of affection, 'We both left home to travel far away.' A comfortable silence fell between them.

'So why d'you leave?' Billy asked.

'It was a dream I had,' she replied, 'a dream I have,' she corrected herself.

The sun was setting fast and the evensong

of kookaburras began to drown out the noise of cicadas grinding rhythmically in the eucalyptus trees. 'Michael never told me you did drugs,' she said watching Billy as he rolled a joint. He laughed, 'God, you make me sound like an addict.' He paused and a shadow, real or imagined, crossed his face, 'it's purely recreational, you know.' He handed her the joint and she lit it and leaned back to relax. 'Nothing wrong with a little attitude adjustment now and then,' Billy continued in a defensive tone.

'Nothing at all,' she agreed, drifting off into a space beyond.

'Jem?'

'Mmm...'

'What's it like? London, I've always wanted to go.'

She looked across the water, thinking about his question. The dying daylight had turned the sky orange with streaks of violet and vermilion. It was spectacular. 'Grey,' she replied, 'dark grey, light grey, different shades of grey, everything's grey; grey skies, grey streets, grey buildings, grey river, grey faces,' but even as she said it a part of her ached for the familiarity of the city which was always in her heart, and which she called home. She saw her mother's smiling face, and she sighed, realising that another week had gone by without speaking to her. She closed her eyes and let go of the day, and thought aloud 'I could sleep for a week.'

There had come a time, she did not know exactly when, when her energy began to wane, not in the natural rhythm that all bodies wax and wane, but in a slow, steady depletion, a seeping out of life force that left jagged, empty holes into which fears and anxieties had crept in.

The more energy she gave to her work, the longer it took her to unwind, and the more drugs or drink she needed to help. This, in turn, led to her digging deep for more energy to achieve the same volume of work, and that left her feeling further depleted. The ever ascending – or was it descending – spiral was making her ill. Her skin was becoming dull and marked, her eyes were scratchy and her hands weren't quite steady. Because she was eating less and smoking more, she had lost weight and become vulnerable to colds and infections. The dark circles under her eyes were becoming more difficult to conceal, even her voice was changing which was especially noticeable in client presentations when she needed to clear her throat before she spoke. The work hard, play hard advertising industry ethic was taking its toll. What began as a 'why not?' now begged the question 'why?' It was a question she did not have the time, nor the inclination to ask herself.

'We always have a choice,' her mother's words echoed faintly in the back of her mind but her mind was now so crowded with other thoughts that she could no longer hear that voice. Nor could she see, because she did not stop long enough to look and because her vision was impaired, the bigger picture.

She had climbed so far, so fast. But where once her imagination was fertile with ideas, now it felt like a wasteland with only thoughts of how to get through each day. That which was full was now empty. At work, each new brief was proving bigger and more difficult to crack than the last, and called for Herculean effort.

'You need a holiday,' Michael said, looking at her as she sat staring blankly across her desk out of the window at the big blue sky.

'I need something,' she replied flatly. There were times lately when he had begun to irritate her. He was always so right, so righteous. Was nothing in his perfect life ever wrong? Did he never get tired, down or depressed?

'Creative review on Project Power tomorrow,'

he said brightly, putting a copy of the week-old brief on her desk. She groaned and turned her head away. She thought of the bag of grass in the tea tin at home. Just one joint would relax her enough to be able to crack that brief. 'I'll be back in an hour,' she said getting up to leave.

'Where are you going?' Michael called after her, but she had gone.

Marijuana made everything right. It ironed out the creases in her mind. It made the crooked paths straight; the cloudy, clear and the rough, smooth. When she was stoned she felt calm and in control, and her imagination soared. She could do anything and everything. Tomorrow. Today, it was sufficient just to let go and release the tension that turned and churned inside her, and give in to the blissful relaxation that washed over her, and quenched her mind like a wave washing over parched sand.

'What are you on?' Michael searched her face for an answer. She giggled. 'You know drugs are for people who can't handle reality,' he said, not for the first time.

'Yeah, yeah,' she retorted, bored with his sanctimonious attitude, 'and reality is for people who can't handle drugs.'

Together, they worked through the brief but it was a struggle. He didn't like her suggestions, and she couldn't follow through on his. The brilliant ideas she had conceived earlier in the day now seemed to be missing something, but she couldn't pinpoint what it was, and Michael didn't know how to tell her – or indeed if he should tell her – that it was simply because there were no ideas, just random, floating thoughts. In the end, they pieced together a campaign whose lack of a central concept was covered up by fashionable words and pictures. It was a cop out. She knew it, he knew it, and they were underestimating the client if they thought they could get away with it.

Night falls quickly in Sydney. From her bed she gazed out of the window at the North Sydney skyline, lit by the neon signs on office blocks. In front of the PHILIPS tower in which she worked flashed an electric blue MAN sign. Amusing, even ironic, she thought, given that her gruelling work schedule prevented her from forming a relationship with any man. It had been a long time, too long, since she'd been close to a man and she lay on her bed, naked, thinking of men, listening to the woman in the flat next door singing as she cooked. Smells of chilli and spices seeped in through the open window but it was too hot to close it, too hot to sleep. She sat upright and rolled a joint and smoked it. Lying back on the bed, she closed her eyes, allowing the marijuana to steal her consciousness, and the restless hours.

It was midnight when she awoke. Too tired to think, too tired to sleep, she felt a pressing need to escape the stultifying confines of her room. One of the agency art directors was hosting a party in a warehouse in Surry Hills, the inner city rag trade district where creative types drank in dimly-lit bars and ate exotic food. She showered, dressed, and gulped down a strong coffee to give her the kick she needed. It was good to get out, to breathe the night and the darkness that only revealed what you wanted to see.

Inside the vast concrete space, a sea of party people swayed to the music of a live band. Sofas were strategically placed near the open windows that looked out onto the night and let in the cool air. In spite of the huge crowd and loud music, the atmosphere was one of relaxed restraint and it felt calm. From the enormous room a doorway led to another room which, when she entered, was quieter. Here, people sat in small groups talking, drinking and smoking. She recognised a colleague from the agency and joined her circle. Sitting cross-legged on the floor, she looked around at the group of people. And that is when she saw him.

Life can be remembered by moments; moments of anger, of peace, moments of separation, of joy. When their eyes locked together, it was one such moment, a moment of complete surrender.

BALANCE

Every runner knows that there is a pace at which you run, a precise speed where your aerobic system is in perfect synchronicity with the energy you expend. It's called the steady state. When you're in the steady state, you move at a pace that feels almost effortless and is so comfortable that you feel like you could run forever. The exact pace depends on the individual and the length of the race, it's slower in a marathon than in a short race. But what doesn't change is the fact that if you run too fast you become exhausted and risk injury to yourself, and if you run too slow you can't keep up. Finding and maintaining that perfect equilibrium, that point of balance between the demands of the race and the output of energy from your body is crucial if you are to have any chance of staying in the race, let alone winning.

The principle of needing to find your 'steady state' becomes especially relevant when you're pitted against the demands of a stressful job, trying to juggle a home and career or plough through a mountain of revision for exams. Your energy is your life force, it's what makes action, doing, possible.

Without energy, the doing becomes impossible. Give too much of yourself and you'll quickly tire and become exhausted. Give too little, and it's likely not to be enough to get the job done.

It takes experience to know when to push forward and when to pull back. And it takes wisdom to know what is worth giving your energy and attention to, and what is not. Clear perspective and judgement, as well as a certain level of detachment is imperative if you are to survive all the demands that life throws at you. 'Don't sweat the small stuff,' said author Richard Carlson, before adding '…and it's all small stuff.'

When you begin to tire, when you find yourself, like a pendulum, swinging fast and slow, high and low, that's the time to slow down. Stop. Understand that moving faster and faster doesn't mean you're achieving what you want. Stop your hurry, curb your impatience and know that time is on your side. Slow your mind, slow your body, and give yourself time, time to rest, time to recharge and renew, so that you can re-enter the race moving better, more efficiently and more balanced. Most of us choose not to make time for ourselves when we need it, instead we give everyone else our time and allow ourselves to run on empty until we run out of energy, lose balance and fall over.

When we feel tired and we want to feel better, we seek help in the least helpful ways. We turn to retail therapy and waste money, we drink too much coffee and eat too much junk food, we stay up late. Sometimes we turn to alcohol or drugs as a remedy, unaware of how they can perpetuate the problem by depleting us of more energy and throwing us further off balance.

There is, of course, a big difference between an occasional social drink and regular indulgence, and although a small amount of alcohol can relax you and make you feel less stressed, it also acts as a depressant of the central nervous system and too much will suppress the part of your brain that controls your judgement. So not only do you feel less energetic, your thinking also loses its edge and you make bad decisions.

The same can be said if you turn to drugs to help you relax, though there are many reasons why you might be drawn to drugs, stress relief being just one. Maybe it's something your friends do and you want to join in. Maybe drugs or alcohol provides an escape, albeit temporarily, from a difficult or painful situation. Maybe you simply want to have fun. No-one wants to deny you pleasure, not at all, but neither drugs nor alcohol are an effective response to your body's call for higher energy levels, and a way to help you feel good. 'Oh, but I do feel good when I've had a drink,' you may say. Or, 'having a smoke is my only pleasure in life.' Pleasure, yes. But joy? Pleasure. Joy. What's the difference? The difference is that pleasure is a transient sensation usually created by external things. Pleasure is not lasting. It disappears as soon the source of the pleasure disappears. The pleasure you feel riding a fairground ride stops when you get off. The pleasure you feel when you're under the influence of alcohol or drugs stops when you sober up.

Joy, on the other hand, is a different sensation, because it comes from a different place. Joy is a deep inner sense of bliss that comes only from within. It is not dependent on outside sources and once you feel it, you can easily recall the feeling. Joy never disappears. How can you tell if what you are feeling is pleasure or joy? One test is to take away the source of pleasure and see if you still feel good. When you feel joy, you can have a bad day, and your joy does not diminish. That's because the source of the joy is within you – it is you.

Without joy, it's easy to mistake pleasure as a good thing. And though the pleasure you get from alcohol and drugs is transitory, the damage caused to your physical, emotional, mental and spiritual health can be permanent.

Quite apart from the physical problems, alcohol and drugs can cause untold harm to your energy flow, and can bring about an abrupt halt to your spiritual development by blocking transmitters and your nervous system.

The Dalai Lama is one of many respected people to speak clearly about the harm caused by taking drugs, 'Although I do not personally have any experience, from talking to people who have taken drugs I have the impression that by taking drugs you lose your discriminative power. This would not be helpful for higher meditation. The mental development should be carried out by internal means, not through external means.'

Your energy is you. It is your life force, and it is the most precious resource you have, more valuable than money or gold. Don't waste it. Spend it wisely. No-one is advocating total abstinence, not unless you want to build the most finely tuned vehicle of a body. When you're young and curious, it's natural that you want to experiment, but it's not a wise move and it's certainly not a prerequisite to becoming an adult. Abstaining, however, is necessary if you are to sustain enough energy to deal with life's daily challenges, let alone a big project or event that requires more energy. You cannot work when you're stoned or drunk, or suffering a hangover. 'I sought pleasure and found Pain. Unutterable,' wrote William Blake in *The First Book of Urizen*. His sentiments were more recently echoed by the legendary Kurt Cobain who, before committing suicide, is reported to have said 'Drugs are a waste of time. They destroy your memory and your self-respect and everything that goes along with your self-esteem.' Even if you have the constitution of an ox, a substance-fuelled existence will take you to a place of self-destruction, where you feel like you're no longer getting on in life, just getting through, where normal everyday pleasures are nothing compared to the pleasure you get from drugs, and where the only way to get on is to get high.

How do you know if you've got a problem? You know you've got a problem when a taste for what you fancy becomes an appetite. When the feeling good is matched by a feeling bad – irritable and agitated – without it. When you need larger amounts to get the same effect. When it stops feeling like fun and starts feeling like a habit. When the more you feed your addiction, the stronger it burns. But mostly, you know you've got a problem when you repeatedly tell yourself that you don't have a problem.

Most alcoholics or addicts-in-waiting partake in this kind of deluded thinking in which they tell themselves that it's okay, everyone's doing it, and they could give it up tomorrow if they wanted. If you find yourself saying or even thinking the same thing, try being honest with yourself, admit you are becoming dependent and choose to do something about it. What should you do? Stop. Easy to say, hard to do.

Maybe you've tried to stop before and not succeeded so now you think you cannot do it. But you know that you must try again. Your body, your mind and your soul knows the truth; the truth that even though what you are doing comes from you, it is not you. It is the truth that retains a sense of perspective and judgement, the truth that fills you with a growing sense of self-loathing, the truth that eventually screams inside you to stop before you completely destroy yourself, the truth that won't go away.

Even when the voice of truth is silent, it is still there, silently disapproving, undermining your pleasure with its painful honesty, and it will stay there until you choose to stop doing whatever it is that is harming you. And though it can be hard, really hard, to beat an addiction, it is not one bit as hard as staying trapped in the thrall of a thing that is sucking the energy and life force out of you. That is much more hard.

Don't ever give up giving up. The next time you give up can be the time you give up for good, the time you take back your strength, your joy, your peace.

There are people who can help you give up and reclaim your life, doctors, counsellors and therapists. And there are things you can do to help yourself. You can help to remove temptation by removing yourself from the people with whom you indulge. Exercise helps, too. Everyone knows that when you exercise you feel good, thanks to the endorphins, the feel-good chemicals that are released into your brain, generating a natural as opposed to an alcohol or drug-induced high. When you take time to take care of your body, your outlook and self-esteem naturally blossom. Sleep is always a welcome antidote to stress and depression. Nourishment is another way to restore your body's strength. When you feed your body good things in place of bad, your energy and vitality returns. No longer are you fanning the flames of a fire that risks burning itself into extinction. Not any more are you out of control, swinging from one extreme to another. Instead, you think clearly and with good judgement, you run at the right pace, you find your steady state, and become perfectly poised, beautifully balanced, ready to take on the world.

As in a race, you have to pace yourself or you won't finish. Be inspired, be passionate, be with the good times, yes. But be aware that a hedonistic lifestyle is at odds with who you really are. When you can maintain this sense of perspective, your judgement becomes clearer and you can keep your mind, your body, and your life in balance.

DESIRE

His long, jet black hair fell into curls over his proud cheekbones and cascaded in waves down his back. He smiled a slow, lazy smile. In a sharp shot of sweet pain, his dancing eyes pierced her soul. She looked away, and looked back. The spell was woven. The magic, cast.

His name was Pangari, the name of a Maori tribal chief from whom he claimed he was descended. Half Maori, half Irish. Half black, half white. Half myth, half man. Half heaven, half hell. She was unaware that he had followed her to the bathroom until she tried to close the door. He pushed his way in and turned the lock. If she was shocked, she didn't protest. He pulled her close and, wordlessly, they fell to the floor, her wine glass smashing against the tiled wall and shattering into a hundred pieces, along with any resistance. Pushing, tugging, crashing into each other, she breathed him in, and the scent of him inflamed her senses.

At one point, he stopped and pulled back. He looked into her and she fell into him, into the abyss, the darkness and the blessed unknown.

In later life she was told that you should never

regret doing anything that makes you smile. If she lived a hundred years she would look back on that moment, and she would smile.

She called him Pan, after the goat-footed nature god, famous for his sexual powers. And after Peter Pan, the boy who never grew up. She could have chosen to say goodbye at that point or indeed at any point, but a passion like that is hard to give up, it makes you yearn for more. And though she sensed it was doomed not to last, she chose to take him home. Now, watching him eat breakfast with the same wild abandon he approached everything, she studied him more closely, the edges of his lips that curled upwards, his crooked teeth, his restlessness, the way he shuffled in his seat. He was too big for the chair, too big for the room, just too big. Like a cat uncomfortable under her gaze, he turned his face away. She wanted to know more. 'But where do you sleep?' she asked. He shrugged his shoulders. No fixed address meant no means of contact, no responsibilities, no questions and definitely no answers. 'Are you with someone else?' He remained silent for a few more seconds. 'It's over,' was all he said.

That evening a black holdall appeared in her

room, and neither of them said a word when she picked it up and put it away in the wardrobe.

It felt good to be bad. She told herself that everyone needs someone like Pan in their life, just once, even though she recognised that he was more potent than any drug, and far more addictive. No matter that it was dangerous. She couldn't remember a time when she had felt so vital and alive.

They would spend whole days together locked inside her room, going out only to buy food at the corner store, or wander through the parks and across the beaches like newcomers to the city who are finding the place, and themselves, for the first time.

They discovered Clovelly, their beach, a small quiet stretch of golden sand framed by large rocks jutting out to sea, in which they could hide from the world. Lying with her head on his chest watching the crashing waves, the fire in her belly burned so strong, it hurt, and he took her to a place where time was no more and nothing else mattered. Afterwards, he waved a scarlet bottlebrush flower gently under her nose, its wiry stamens tickling her. 'Where to tonight?' he asked. She thought about it.

'Well, if you don't have any friends,' she paused, 'then you must meet mine.'

'Killer eyes,' said Billy watching Pan jump from the balcony of the boathouse into the water and surface, shaking his long hair. 'Or maybe just killer?' Billy turned to look at her questioningly. She looked down at Pan swimming naked, and smiled,

'Maybe.'

'Seriously, he should come with a government health warning: this man can damage your health,' Billy was concerned.

'Speaking of health,' she changed the subject, 'you look tired. You okay?'

Billy lit a cigarette and coughed. 'Fine,' he said, and opened another cold can of beer.

She was happy to introduce Pan to Billy but, for reasons she could not fathom, not Michael. As far as the agency was concerned, she was suffering from exhaustion and was taking a holiday. No-one seemed to mind and if they did, she didn't care. It was not that her work was no longer important, nor that she had absolved all responsibility towards it. It was just that whenever she thought of work her head hurt. It was as if her brain was stuck in first gear and she couldn't shift it forward, or pick up any speed.

Together, she and Pan played out the last of the

summer days, cooled by the southerly wind that had gathered strength and whispered of the storm to come. He had taken to disappearing now and then, sometimes not returning until the following day. During those times, her body ached with longing and her mind became crippled with thoughts of him with someone else.

When he came home, which he eventually always did, she would feed him and bathe him and love him. He would lighten the mood by doing a Maori Haka where he would open his eyes and mouth wide and stick out his tongue. She later learned that this is a sign of contempt. But right now, he made her laugh. He also made her cry, with fear that she might be losing him. Yet she would willingly trade one hundred tears for one more night together.

One day, he returned home, from where she did not ask, more agitated than usual. He didn't want her love, he wanted to take her out. He knew a place, he said, a new club on George Street that had just opened and was serving free drinks.

They entered through an unassuming doorway and at the top of a tall, narrow staircase, behind a reception desk, a smartly dressed Asian woman smiled, not so sweetly, as Pan paid the entrance fee which she thought was unusual, given that he never paid for anything. Once inside the bar, they found a comfortable leather sofa in the corner and a young waitress, also Asian, served them glasses of champagne from a tray. Apart from the soft background music and the tinkling of glasses at the bar, it was quiet, and she relaxed into the sofa, glad to be here with him in this welcoming room, glad that he wanted to take her out and that he wanted to spend this time together.

She stroked his hand and turned to kiss him but was interrupted by the waitress who had returned with two thick white towelling robes. She was puzzled, 'Have they got a pool?' she asked him, but he didn't answer. Carrying the robes, he took her hand and led her away from their private space, down a darkened corridor with many doorways leading off and one, at the end, that led into a large, dark room.

It took a few seconds for her eyes to adjust to the darkness, and when they did she was taken aback at what she saw; a rolling sea of bodies, luminescent and naked, writhing around on the floor. Everywhere, people were having sex, men and women, men and men. She felt her throat tighten and her stomach churn as she stood motionless in the doorway. She looked at Pan, speechless, but he did not look at her, he scanned the room and, still holding her hand, he led her in. And she followed.

Slowly, he lay her down, and unzipped her dress. He didn't look at her face, if he had, he would have seen her gazing at him through eyes filled with tears and sorrow as everything became painfully clear. He didn't want her, he wanted to share her, she was his ticket to a good time. Without her, he was not allowed in this place. That was what the sign said at reception, that was the rule: *'Women welcome. Men welcome only if accompanied by a woman.'* It didn't make sense then, but now its meaning was clear. Everything was clear. Perfectly, pitifully, painfully clear.

He leaned down to kiss her and she turned her head away. He had tricked her. Or had he? Was she not a willing victim? Did she not go along with everything he ever wanted, without question? She had needed no persuading to walk into his web and now she needed to summon all her strength of mind and heart to walk out. She felt his hands caress her body, and then she felt the hands of a stranger. She moaned softly, not with pleasure but with pain. This is not me. The thought came from somewhere deep inside her. If she was no longer sure of who she was, she was at least sure of who she was not, and she was not the person he now wanted her to be. This is not me, the voice inside her spoke louder. And she moved, slowly at first, then with determination, to the door.

She waited for him at the bar and they left in silence. She wanted to cry, to shout at him, to hit him, but she did none of these things. She simply stared into the empty blackness of the night. A taxi drove them home over the Harbour Bridge and she turned, as she always did, to look across at the Opera House, its gleaming white sails illuminated against the velvet sky. She leaned out of the open window, and the wind blew through her hair and washed her face and she opened her mouth, gulping in the cold air, feeling it hit the back of her throat, and it felt good. She opened her mouth wider and inhaled deeper, the air raced through her, filling her up and from nowhere, or somewhere, she howled a primeval howl, like a wounded animal, calling the night.

The bond had been broken, the spell, undone. The next morning, he was gone. It ended the same way it had begun, swiftly, and without words. She was surprised not by his departure, only by how much it hurt. There was no consolation in telling herself that she knew this day would come. She had always known that he would never be hers. You don't own someone like Pan. They pass through your life like the southerly buster, stirring up emotions lying deep in your soul, and leaving behind them a trail of scattered debris.

Nor did she feel better for knowing that it was she who was ultimately responsible for what had happened, for she had wittingly made this choice. She had invited him into her life, into her bed, and into her heart. Fuelled by desire, she had flown her plane like a Kamikaze pilot towards its target, and certain death. 'Michael?' she held the phone tightly, and tried to sound light and happy.

'How are you?' his voice was soft and gentle.

'How's work?'

'Busy. When are you coming back?'

DESIRE

The burning heat, the quickening heart, the look that lingers, the longing, the madness, the surrender to the thing that is desire. 'Desire is half of life; indifference is half of death,' wrote the philosopher, Kahil Gibran. Surely there are few times when you feel more alive than when you are in the grip of desire.

Whether desire creeps up behind you and takes you unawares or charges straight at you, its effects are the same: conflicting, paradoxical emotions that carry you on a roller coaster ride, soaring to the highest heights and plunging to the deepest depths. One day, complete fulfilment, the next, emptiness and despair.

Desire makes you care more and careless. It inflames your heart and invades every pathway in your mind. When you want someone so bad, it's impossible to concentrate on anything else. A shift in control moves, seismically, away from yourself to the other person and you find yourself at their mercy. Will he, won't he? Does she, doesn't she? The torment, the wanting that won't go away, the passion. But desire is not passion. And passion is not desire. No, passion is something else.

Passion is how you express your perfect Self. It is what leads you to action, to create, to do. Passion gets you up in the morning and keeps you awake at night. Passion drives you to write one more line, paint one more stroke, compose one more bar, mend one more machine, sew one more stitch. Passion lies at the heart of your finest achievements. You cannot deny your passion, nor should you. Desires, though, are not always best pursued.

If passion is what drives you, if it is the river running through your life, then desire can be described as the moorings along the way, the points at which you can choose to disembark, or sail straight past. You cannot stop the river – your passion, but you can always choose not to stop and act on your desires.

There's the rub. Do you choose to fall for the person or object of your desires and fly willingly, eagerly, like a moth into the dancing flame, headlong into trouble and the certainty that you will be burned? Or, do you choose to save your sanity and summon all your strength and walk away from a desire that does not serve you well?

Since time began there have been irresistible men and women who have held the promise of wild adventure. You see them everywhere, in books, in paintings, in stories in newspapers, sitting in the corner of your local pub, standing on the railway platform, or delivering the mail.

Every Casanova, male and female, knows only too well how to seduce you with a sexually charged invitation that triggers an adrenalin rush like no other and before you've had time to pick your brain up from the floor, you have fallen into a relationship that is as unpredictable as it is dangerous.

'Ahaa,' you say with a smile, 'but the sex, the physical attraction is worth every minute of anguish spent waiting in vain for him or her to call.' Maybe it is. Maybe just once, yes, the pleasure is worth the pain. Maybe, possibly, even twice. But if you find yourself continually attracted, even addicted to relationships based only on great sex, you need to question something.

Sex can be the most exciting, enlightening, extraordinary experience. As our species means of procreation, it is our most basic and urgent primal urge and the underlying cause of many of our thoughts and actions.

Sex is also possibly the most powerful energy we have. With or without our consciousness, sex drives our behaviour, affecting both insignificant and important things we do. Sex can create and sex can destroy. Sex can transform and transcend. It knows no boundaries, no limits, it knows no 'no', it takes you to a place where everything else dissolves and nothing else matters. Sex is the beginning, and the end. The French expression for the shift in consciousness that lovers experience after orgasm is *le petit mort* – the little death.

Yet no matter how strong the sexual charge you feel with someone, the strength of that attraction can and will diminish. Where love can last forever, desire lasts just a couple of months. And the person you meet and immediately have sex with is rarely the person you live with happily ever after.

Because your sexual energy is so powerful, and because it's such an integral part of you, it's vital that you channel your sexual energy properly. Of course there are also physical reasons why you need to be cautious and take precautions, but what is less known is what happens to you on a non-physical level when you have sex with someone.

Anyone who has seen Kirlian photography of the electric field – the aura – that surrounds all living beings, knows that the colours of the aura range from murky browns to clear and brilliant colours, depending on the health of the individual.

This high voltage photography reveals that the field of energy around the body is especially sensitive to its immediate environment and changes colour accordingly. Even a simple handshake or kiss changes the aura.

Given that there is no way of getting physically closer to someone than by having sex, you can imagine the enormous and often violent changes to your aura that take place during sex. For better or worse, your energy field absorbs that of your partner and disturbs your entire being.

If you have sex with someone you hardly know, you are drawing unknown energies into yourself – anger, fear, jealousy, guilt, who knows what else – any one of which can harm you mentally and emotionally. If you continue to have sex with people you do not know, or use sex as a means of getting close to someone, you risk doing real harm to your Self.

In his book *Aura, Shield of Protection & Glory*, Torkom Saraydarian describes how parts of your aura can become 'dislocated' due to overuse of certain practices, including sex, and how this affects you, 'Dislocation sometimes occurs slowly when continuous attention is given to certain locations such as the sex organs. Sometimes the mental body corrects itself; sometimes it cannot... Each time dislocation occurs, a person comes closer to losing his stability. This condition affects logic, creates confusion, light-headedness, absentmindedness and insanity.'

Excessive sex over a long period of time drains your aura and disturbs your thinking. When you have sex with a stranger you're exposing yourself to all sorts of potential problems and conditions that can hurt you not just physically but mentally and emotionally, too. But what happens when two people love each other? How does that change the quality of your sex and its effect on your mind and body?

If you love someone who loves you in return and if you abstain from sex for a while, you will discover that the love energy between you deepens. It's a beautiful feeling, a 'sure' feeling that induces a sense of calm not craziness. Instead of feeling desperate, you feel stable and complete. Instead of feeling fearful, you feel in control. And when the two of you finally do have sex together, all your positive energy blends to heighten and expand the experience, and its after effects.

Sexual energy is creative energy. When you think about its purpose, how could it not be?

This is something that every artist, composer and creative thinker understands, and feels. When you abstain, at least temporarily, your sexual energy is sublimated and your aura becomes highly charged and magnetic. Your mental strength increases and you find yourself far better equipped to create truly creative and beautiful work.

No-one is suggesting you stop having sex altogether – although many people do choose to become celibate and channel their sexual energy into their work – but what is clear is that if you continually give yourself away sexually, you risk damaging yourself in ways that may leave you permanently scarred.

It's easy, especially when you're young, to believe that happiness depends on finding a partner, someone who will love you as much as you love them. It's easy too to hand over control of your happiness to someone else without even realising that you're doing so.

We look for approval from others often because we don't know how to approve of ourselves. Attention from the opposite sex can boost your self-esteem, it can make you feel good, make you feel wanted, and make it easier to fall into bed with someone. Only later, when that person has left, do you realise that they didn't really want you, they wanted sex, and the feeling good now feels like abandonment. It's easy then to pretend that you feel nothing when what you really feel is hurt and anger. Easy to indulge in a series of empty one night stands, refusing to admit that you want something more, or are worth a whole lot better.

'Don't compromise yourself, you're all you've got,' said rock singer, Janis Joplin who in spite of, or perhaps because of, the fact that she compromised herself a great deal, understood the value of acting in a way that is respectful and honourable to yourself.

Lack of self-esteem often goes back to childhood when how you felt about yourself was a direct reflection of how your parents felt about you. If you felt unloved, you learned that you are not worthy of love. If you were not treated with respect, you learned that you do not deserve respect. If, however, you were cherished and cared for, you know how to nurture yourself and know, too, that you deserve to be loved.

Maybe you grew up without a parent and you had to learn how to love by yourself, which no child can do. If this is so, you may unwittingly be wanting a partner to replace a parent in which case the relationship has little chance of lasting.

Abandonment, neglect, abuse, whatever the reason, whatever the story behind your lack of self-love, you need to deal with any negative beliefs you may have about yourself if you are to learn to love and respect yourself. Because it's only when you love and respect yourself can you expect someone else to love and respect you. Only when you believe you are beautiful, can someone else see your beauty. Only when you know you are worthy of a loving, long lasting relationship will you attract someone who wants the same.

It starts with you. Don't be in a hurry to give yourself away, not to anyone, no matter how attractive they are, or what promises they hold. Would you give away a precious piece of jewellery you owned to someone you hardly knew? Would you hand over someone you love to someone you didn't know? Of course not. Why then give away your body? Yet many people treat themselves as if they are not worthy of the same care, attention and respect they give to others, or even their own belongings. They, often without realising it, hurt themselves and a sure way to hurt yourself is to give yourself physically (and in any other way) to someone who doesn't really respect you, let alone love you.

Take back your body, take back your mind, take back your heart, take back your Self. Stop what you're doing and take it all back. The moment you do so, you take back your power. Then you can start to give yourself all the love and respect you deserve. If you find it hard to love yourself, try at least respect; treat yourself with the same level of respect and care that you would someone – or something – you love. If even self-respect feels uncomfortable, talk to a professional therapist or counsellor who can help you overcome your lack of self-esteem.

You are the answer to you. You must feel good about yourself first before you can feel good about someone else. You are responsible for your own happiness and joy. When you do what is good for you, your goodness grows and others will be drawn to you like a magnet.

Understand, too, that just because you desire someone physically doesn't mean you have to act on that desire. 'The secret of happiness is to admire without desiring,' said American writer Carl Sandberg.

Pause for just a moment's thought and you may see that, as much as you want a person, he or she will make you unhappy. You may be physically attracted to someone but unless you both want the same thing emotionally, the relationship has little chance of lasting. Realise that you cannot change another person. The only person you can change is yourself. Why not, instead, choose to admire the person of your desire, as you would admire any other object of beauty, a work of art, for example. Step back, appreciate its beauty and, in the full awareness that you cannot afford – emotionally, physically and mentally – to buy it, walk away.

'Pleasure without conscience' is one of Mahatma Gandhi's 'Seven Sins in the World'. The other six, incidentally, are: Wealth without work, knowledge without character, commerce without morality, science without humanity, worship without sacrifice, and politics without principle.

You can work at changing your desires, choosing desires that are compatible with what you want for yourself and your future, choosing those that are healthy and positive, and make you feel bigger not smaller,

If you desire someone but you hear alarm bells, do not ignore them. Face the truth and don't talk yourself into believing something is more than it really is. People do fall in love at first sight but it's usually far too soon to know if what you feel is true.

Many young women and men sleep with lots

of partners, believing it is evidence that they are loved. Sex can feel wonderfully close and it's easy to assume that other parts of the relationship are as close, easy to think that because you are connected physically, you are also connected emotionally. But just because you wish for something to be a certain way doesn't make it so, and if you believe that sex without love is anything more than just that, you are fooling yourself. The more you fool yourself, the harder it becomes to leave and find a mutually loving relationship.

When you fall under the magical spell of sex, it's easy to confuse it with love. But love is not sex. And sex is not love.

How do you know if it is love? Listen to the voice within you, the voice that tells you whether something or someone is good or bad, right or wrong. Listen to the voice, trust the voice and follow it. It is your heart. The Irish have a proverb: 'Your feet will bring you to where your heart is.'

Believe that your heart will lead you to the right person, and to love. Do not pretend that love is not what you are looking for. Love is what everyone is looking for. In your heart, you know that love is far richer than sex. And when your feet have brought you to your heart, you will stand tall and relaxed, glowing with the colours of the rainbow, love streaming out of you, and you will know that it was worth the work. It was worth the wait.

ACCEPT

There is no autumn in Sydney. Summer trips into winter and suddenly everyone's talking about the rain and cold, and whether or not they should wear a coat. Under thick grey skies, the harbour moves to a slower rhythm. And so did she. Slowly, gently, she picked up her bruised heart and returned to work. With the edges of her memory slightly blurred, she found it difficult at first to keep pace with the demands of her job. Michael helped, like Michael always helped, and she accepted his kindness and patience as she re-entered the real world.

He watched her as she sat silently staring blankly at a notepad on her lap, doodling instead of writing. 'Whoever he was, Jem, he wasn't worth it,' he said, probing for information. She looked up in sharp defence. Billy must have told him about Pan, that was clear. But she didn't want to reveal anything to him about that relationship, or what she was now feeling, though in truth she wasn't feeling much at all.

She was trying not to dwell on what had gone, rather, accept that she and Pan were finished and she would never see him again. He had claimed her body and her heart and, for a brief time, her mind. Now she must free herself from his invisible hold on her and move forward. She was no longer feeling angry nor even sad, she was just feeling a kind of dull emptiness and this was why she was quiet and withdrawn; it was her way (as it is most people's way) of transforming the anger and hurt into acceptance and healing. 'I know,' she replied rather sharply and sat up straight, 'So, what you do you think…' her eyes lit up mischievously as she picked up the brief for a television commercial from her desk, '…open on wide shot of desert island?'

The music was loud, the chattering among the guests even louder. Michael had insisted that she come to their party and since he and Sunny, too, were intent on pulling her out of her room and into some kind of social life, she obliged. Besides, they were right, she knew that she needed to find a better balance between work and play, and meeting new people would help. Now, with the music thumping above the convivial laughter, she wished she had stayed home. She had always felt lonely in a crowd, but never more so than now. A man, good looking and aware of his charms, caught her attention and smiled. She looked away embarrassed and anxious, too, at how the encounter triggered the still sore wound inside her, but it was too late. The next moment he was by her side chatting about something and nothing, and asking her questions that she didn't want to answer. She regarded him with suspicion, he didn't fool her. She knew what he was. She spotted Sunny gliding across the room, filling up people's glasses from a bottle of champagne. Unapologetically, Jem walked away and towards Sunny's side.

'Where's Billy?' she asked Sunny, wishing he were there.

'Isn't he here? He said he was coming.'

'I might go and get him,' she replied, looking for an excuse to leave.

'Oh, please don't go yet – stay, we've something important to say!' The normally serene Sunny was almost delirious with excitement. And before they even announced their engagement to the room, Jem knew what was coming. She clapped and cheered along with everyone else, yet she wondered why she didn't feel the happiness that she knew she should for Sunny and Michael, her friends, who were made for each other.

What was it that she felt? Envy? Resentment? If Michael was her friend (at times she believed, saviour), why did she not share his happiness? Did she feel more for him than friendship? She looked across the crowded room at him, animated in conversation, stroking his hair, as he so often did in a futile attempt to flatten his fringe, and something inside her heart tugged and pulled and made her feel uncomfortable, and she cursed her imagination and her dark thoughts as she picked up her bag and headed for the door.

Red could be heard barking from far off, warning her that all was not as it should be and as she raced down the 101 stone steps she almost tripped and fell. 'Billy!' she shouted, running up to the door which, as usual, was unlocked. Inside, Billy was lying on the floor, not far from the phone with its receiver dangling. She knelt down beside him, shouting his name and he opened his eyes. His breathing was strained and when he tried to speak, he couldn't. She grabbed the phone and called for an ambulance.

'Acquired Immune Deficiency Syndrome. AIDS. That's what the doctors call it. I call it a punishment.' He sat upright in the hospital bed, and despite the plastic tubes protruding from his body he looked, she thought, remarkably well. It was less than 24 hours since he'd been admitted into St Vincent's and diagnosed with a severe chest infection. Now, his breathing had steadied and with the help of an oxygen mask he was able to speak, at least short sentences.

She had heard of AIDS, it was a new disease, so new that not everyone knew how it was transmitted and there were a lot of untruths being circulated, creating some hysteria among people who were ignorant and fearful of how they might catch it, and what it might do. Ignorance and fear is a dangerous combination.

In years to come, AIDS would become the term that doctors would use to describe the latter stages of the Human Immunodeficiency Virus (HIV), a virus that attacks the body's immune system. But now, AIDS was what Billy had, and not even the doctors could yet understand the exact nature of the virus, or how best to treat it. What they did know was that it was especially prevalent in the homosexual community and Sydney was Australia's epicentre of the disease. Only last week the State Health Department had commissioned Dermot, McMasters and Mills to produce a cross-media educational campaign on what AIDS was, and what it was not and, in a synchronous twist of fate, she and Michael were one of the teams who had been chosen to work on the campaign.

'I know what it is,' she paused. 'It's not a punishment.'

'It's a death sentence,' he said, in a dry, matter of fact tone. And she squeezed his hand, knowing that what he said was probably true, and not knowing what she could say to make it better.

They agreed that he – and Red – would go home, to Mungerannie. It was not the ideal choice, but she couldn't look after him full time and he preferred that his mother did so rather than the nurses, some of whom were less than kind to him. No, it was far better that he was cared for with love and with understanding by his mother who, it transpired, knew of his illness and had steeled herself for this time. What his mother did not know, however, was that he and his 'friend' Jem were officially man and wife. 'That'll bloody rock 'em,' Billy chuckled, 'Poofta son got married!' No matter how much she'd grown to love him (and she had), she could not become accustomed to his acerbic, self-deprecating way.

The winter clouds piled high on the horizon

and she sat on a bench at Kirribilli Wharf from where not even the sight of the picture book ferries chugging in and out of Circular Quay across the harbour could lift her spirit.

Billy was sick, seriously sick and she had no idea how long he might live. Michael and Sunny were to be wed, and that sealed the end to any possible future – or love – she might imagine she had with him. Her work, despite offering her the freedom and creativity she sought, was not the work she had dreamed of. Nor was her home one little bit like that which she had so carefully crafted in her imagination, the vision of which had led her across the world. In fact her dream, when she thought about it, was so far removed from her reality that it physically hurt too much to think about it. But she knew that think about it was what she had to do, no matter how unpalatable or difficult it was. This was one of many lessons that her mother had taught her. 'Life is difficult, Jem,' she would say when what she experienced was not what she wanted, 'the moment you accept that and get on with it, it becomes less difficult.'

'I am alone,' she said to herself, 'and lonely.' And she felt a shiver run through her, awakening her body that was stiff from sitting still. The damp air was blowing in from the Pacific bringing the evening's first spots of rain. The thought of going home alone was too depressing. She stood up and put one foot in front of the other and kept walking until she arrived at the door to her office where Michael was working late. He looked up as she sat down.

'Have you heard from Billy?' she asked.

'Yes,' he put down his pencil and his expression was one of quiet acceptance. 'I want to do something to help, but I don't know what.'

'Nor me,' she replied, 'We can go and visit him,' she suggested, 'at his parents' place – soon.'

'Yes, yes of course,' he seemed to cheer up at this thought. 'Would you like to go for a drink?' he asked, reading her mind.

They found a table in the corner of the pub. There were many things that she wanted to say to him but instead she said what she thought was right, 'I never got to congratulate you on your engagement. Cheers!' she raised her glass.

'Cheers,' Michael echoed, smiling.

'To Billy,' she said, quietly.

'Yes, to Billy.' echoed Michael, embarrassed that, for a few moments, he had escaped their attention.

A silence fell upon them, she looked down at her badly bitten fingernails and turned her hands over.

'Shall we get something to eat?' He interrupted her thoughts. Yes, she would like that, more than anything right now, to sit with him and share a meal, to maybe tell him how she might feel in the hope that maybe he felt the same. But she knew that was not going to happen, and she was so tired of maybes and mights. It was that kind of thinking that dreams were made of and dreams, she was beginning to believe, were dangerous things. Dreams didn't get you anywhere.

'No. Thank you. I'd like another drink, though.' Another drink would blot out the day. But she noticed that, though the alcohol did its job, it didn't taste so good. And when Michael left to go home to Sunny, she drank more, not caring what anyone who watched her might think, not caring what she felt or didn't feel, just feeling sad, and drunk, and alone.

When she arrived back at her room, she couldn't find her key. She searched through her bag and searched again. She tipped it upside down and her purse, make-up, cigarettes, everything fell out noisily onto the tiled floor, everything except her key. She banged on the door, though why, she did not know, no-one was there. It was an act of desperation. She slumped to the floor, the cool tiles felt good against her flushed skin. Maybe it was the result of too much alcohol, too little sleep, or the exertion of climbing all those stairs, but it felt wonderful to lie down, just for a minute she told herself, and take in the cold comfort of the stone floor. The door to the room next to hers quietly opened, and an old woman peered out at her.

'I've lost my key,' she said, looking up at the stranger, not stirring.

'Flamin' full moon,' said the woman disapprovingly, and disappeared back inside her room to fetch the spare key that the previous tenant had given her.

After mumbling her thanks to her neighbour, she crashed into her room, and into bed. The last thing she heard before she fell asleep was the sound of the rain beating against the window. When it rains in Sydney, it rains hard.

ACCEPT

'Honesty is the first chapter in the book of wisdom,' said American President Thomas Jefferson, two hundred years ago. Being honest with yourself though can be one of the most difficult things to do. But being honest with yourself is exactly what you need to be when you fall into a situation, or behave in a way that is destructive or damaging. The expression 'You can run, but you can't hide' rings especially true when you try to run away from your own problems.

Of course you can – and possibly will – try to run away from your problem. It take maturity and strength to admit you are wrong. And the mind is adept at twisting the truth when it wants to. But if you do this, the problem will simply follow you around, never leaving your side until you deal with it. Like a weed in the garden, if you ignore a problem, it continues to grow. Dealing with a problem means taking a long hard look at yourself and facing up to the reality of the situation. It means being completely honest with yourself, no matter how difficult that is, and accepting yourself, and your situation for what it is. It means considering how you may be hurting yourself, or another, or if you are allowing someone else to hurt you.

It seems unimaginable that with all the wisdom and understanding we have accrued, we can still so readily hurt ourselves to the point of self destruction.

When we behave in this way, we can no longer hear our inner voice or attempt to overcome our suffering and pain. We go into denial.

Yet the most incredible thing happens when you acknowledge your inner voice. It becomes clear and loud. Something almost magical takes place as soon as you accept you have a problem.

Everything changes.

How often are we told that 'accepting you have a problem is the first step to solving it.' Self-acknowledgement is a powerful force. When you accept something for what it truly is, you can change it. Always, before change comes acceptance.

This is why acceptance is so empowering and not, as some might say, weak. Far from it, acceptance is when you stop pretending something is what it isn't, you stop fooling yourself, and you embrace the truth and take action – no matter how difficult or painful it is. Actually the pain you feel when you are honest with yourself is a good pain, because it is the truth and the truth always feels right. 'There is no negotiation with truth' said German socialist, Ferdinand Lassalle. The moment you accept the truth, you feel an almost immediate sense of relief and peace that you can never experience when you're deluding yourself.

Once you accept the truth and stop fighting or resisting it, everything becomes easier. The intense conflict you felt vanishes, everything becomes clear and starts to flow again and you are no longer swimming against the tide of truth.

Be kind in your acceptance. Don't criticise or judge yourself – or others. There is no point in giving yourself a hard time by reliving a situation, or wishing you had done things differently. You cannot change what has happened, just as you cannot change another person. But you can alter how you are going to respond to a problem now, and tomorrow.

There are many times in your life when you need to withdraw, to be quiet, to take stock and wait for the right moment to re-enter the game of life. This is one such time. Author, Franz Kafka beautifully summed up this important time of acceptance, of inaction before action, when he wrote, 'You do not need to leave your room, remain sitting at your table and listen. Do not even listen, simply wait. Do not even wait, be quite still and solitary. The world will freely offer itself to you to be unmasked, it has no choice. It will roll in ecstasy at your feet.'

Often at a time that precedes a great turning point in your life, you find that the right person comes knocking on your door, the right book falls off the shelf or the right opportunity is presented to you as a gift. You also feel that a huge, irreversible change is taking place deep within you.

It takes courage and maturity to accept things for what they really are instead of what you want them to be. When you find that courage you are likely to feel anxious. Indeed, the bigger the change the more anxious you may feel. Know that this feeling is temporary, as it accompanies the moment of transition from non-acceptance to acceptance. Any feelings of anxiety are completely natural, and are a part of the process of change.

In his book *Divine Beauty*, John O'Donohue likens this time to 'coming through a hidden door into a bright field of springtime that we could have never discovered otherwise.' He goes on to say 'Now could be the most important moment in life to steel our courage and enter the risk of change. Meister Eikhart says: 'Stand still and do not waver from your emptiness; for at this time you can turn away, never to turn back again.'

Be strong, be courageous, accept your situation and your role in it. The moment you do so, you will be rewarded with a deep, unwavering peace – the kind of peace that will never desert you. Peace, real peace, is a feeling that comes from within not without. And when you possess that kind of peace, you can change your world. And your life.

CHOOSE

Short and plain, she was the far side of sixty, but her eyes – and her tongue – were as sharp as a tack. She carried with her a faintly antiseptic smell, and though you wouldn't look twice at her walking down the street, Gloria King was one of a kind. Gloria talked to the stars. And the stars talked back.

Her room – the only other room on the top floor – was a jumble of books, magazines, papers and pictures crammed into bulging mahogany bookcases and piled up on a large round wooden table and on every available inch of worn Persian carpet. There were plenty of other things, too, wonderful and weird objects that lined the shelves around the room; stones and crystals, feathers of all colours and sizes, framed sepia photos of old people, crucifixes, statues of Hindu gods and other religious icons and on the window sill, a collection of tiny glass bottles that reflected the dull winter's light.

Papering the walls were pictures of saints, their auras aglow, as well as all kinds of pictures of all types of angels, biblical angels, animal angels, chubby cherub angels, romantic renaissance angels,

African and Indian angels. Angels everywhere. One angel in particular caught her eye. Tall, blonde and muscular, his wings were enormous, bigger than he, and he was adorned in an iridescent blue cloak. In his hand he carried a gleaming sword, its blade as sharp as his wings were soft. When she looked at the picture, she could almost feel the warmth of his wings wrapped around her, protecting her.

Elsewhere in the room was a single bed, neatly made, two wooden chairs and a screen that, like the one in her own room, hid the kitchen area. When she sat down, she felt that she were the centrepiece in a museum display. Some might say that Gloria herself was a museum piece, but Jem thought differently. In the very short time since they had become acquainted the two women, more different you could not meet, had struck up a friendship.

Gloria looked up from the piece of paper on which she had drawn an astrological chart, a circle divided into sections, like a pie. Inside each section she had written numbers and strange glyphs. 'Voltaire said that each player must accept the cards that life deals him or her,' she explained, 'but once they are in hand, he or she alone must decide how to play the cards in order to win the game,' she continued, 'Think of the planets as like the cards in your hand. Depending on how they are placed in your birth chart, they are strong, or weak. And how you play them is up to you.'

She listened intently to the older woman's explanation. 'You were born with Neptune on the ascendant, the sign of a dreamer.' She got that right. 'It can be your downfall. Or your salvation.' Gloria looked up and felt a surge of compassion for the girl, who she could see was lost and searching for answers. She continued, 'Astra inclinant, non necessitant – the stars impel us, they do not compel us. You always have a choice, Jem.'

She was struck silent by Gloria's words, the same words that her mother had been repeating to her for years. She did not need to be a mystic to realise that it was a message that she must heed. 'Choice?' she questioned. The kettle was whistling on the stove. Gloria continued talking as she rose from the table to make tea. 'We make choices every minute of the day, the mundane – will you have a ginger nut with your tea? And the meaningful – will you change the course of your life, and your destiny?'

'You can change your destiny?'

'You can choose to run away from your destiny.' Gloria looked at her questioningly, 'Many do. Or you can choose to follow your destiny, play the game.'

Gloria paused, reading her uncertainty and confusion, 'no matter how difficult it gets.'

'How do you know if you are following your destiny?'

'Your heart will tell you.' Gloria replied, and then added, 'Listen to your heart.' And because the older woman had, again, spoken the same words of her mother, she knew her words were true, and that she must heed them.

It is difficult to listen to your heart when so many other voices inside you are screaming for attention. She realised she had reached a nadir, and with that realisation came an unexpected sense of calm. She decided she would no longer tear herself to pieces, plagued by the thought that she was failing to make her dream come true. She would, no more, fight against others, or herself, for a dream that may or may not materialise. She felt no struggle, no resistance, no desperate wanting, no needing. She felt only a wave of peace wash over her, leaving in its wake a clean and blissfully pure sense of equilibrium.

She acknowledged that she could not change

what had happened. Nor could she change other people or their affections towards her. But she could change herself. And she resolved that from this point forward, she would work to change the things about herself that did not fit the image of the person she wanted to be, the person her heart told her she was.

There would be no drugged and drunken nights. No more sex with strangers. No more battles. She chose, at that moment, to take control of her mind and body. And in so doing, she chose to follow her destiny.

It was a brave decision. But then her bravery was never in doubt, for only a person of courage would have come this far. The courageous take responsibility for their own lives. They make decisions in the full awareness that they have been given the gift of choice and the ability to determine their future. The problems, the obstacles, the setbacks, the pain and hurt that confront them are not indiscriminate punishments, they are challenges to be overcome, or not.

She could see clearly that where she was now was a result of the choices she had made. And that she, and only she, could take responsibility for her actions, past and present. Taking responsibility did not mean following rules laid down by another. It meant writing her own rules, working out for herself what action to take to move her closer to the dream of who she wanted to be.

As is usual with important personal turning points, there was no celebration or applause to accompany the momentous decision she had made. There was instead the quiet, calm acknowledgement that she – and her life – was about to change.

When she returned to her room there was a message from her mother on the answerphone. Her voice sounded confused at having to speak into the newfangled machine and it held a tinge of tiredness, or maybe it was impatience for it had been a long time since they had spoken. Thinking about her mother, the phone rang again.

'Mum?'

'Darling! How are you?'

She apologised to her mother for being a less than dutiful daughter, before going on to tell her, briefly, about the events of the last few months; how Billy was taken ill (she did not explain why), how her neighbour had become her friend, (she did not tell her how they first met), how Michael was getting married (she did not discuss her feelings towards him). Mostly, though, she did not dwell on the past, because she wanted to leave the past behind. She talked instead about what she was doing right now. And, like all daughters, and sons too, she told her mother what she thought her mother wanted to hear; that she was taking better care of her health, she was developing a more responsible attitude towards her work, she was finding new friends and discovering new meaning to the world.

She did not talk about following her dream, she did not need to. Her mother knew her daughter well, and she knew that she would always carry her dream, for nothing is ever lost, and her mother knew that such dreams never die, they just sometimes become buried under the burdens of life.

Indeed, her mother did not say much at all. She listened. And at the end of the conversation, she asked only one question:

'Are you happy, darling?'

'Yes,' she replied, comforted by the fact that her happiness, her life, was cherished by her mother, the way all mothers cherish the happiness of their children. And, though she was not convinced that what she was feeling was true happiness, hearing her mother's voice and feeling her mother's love induced a more serene and positive approach to life.

For the first time in a long time she felt in control of her own destiny. From now on, she would do only good things for herself, and for others. She phoned Billy who was settling in well at his parents' home, grumbling about the food and the heat and they agreed that she would come and visit very soon.

Thinking about Billy, she wandered onto her balcony and sat on a chair, taking in the view of the North Sydney skyline. She thought how, but for the hand of fate (or was it in the stars?) it could so easily have been her, not him, to catch this new virus. For in their wanting to be loved, she and Billy were alike. She, too, had craved the attention of another and had fallen for the misbelief that giving herself away was proof that she was loved. And, like Billy, she had come close to abandoning all reason. For what? Love? Lust? Desire? If that was a crime (and she could never believe that it was) then being struck with a fatal, incurable disease seemed an unduly harsh punishment.

Thinking about Billy, she reflected on how one moment can change a life forever. She thought it incongruous that in this age you could die from giving yourself to another. She wanted to make it better but was lost as to what she could do to help.

The daylight was fast fading and across the freeway, the signs atop the tower blocks of North Sydney began to light up the horizon, yellow, red and green. Staring into the sky beyond the building in which she worked, the answer came to her, not slowly, but fast like a thunderbolt. There was no gradual build up of an idea, no tossing back and forth of a notion. There was, instead, a precise and unmistakably clear message, one that was straight in front of her. North Sydney. Agency. Work. Brief. The message was clear and loud. She would write the AIDS campaign. She and Michael would create a piece of communication that would capture everyone's attention, a campaign that clearly, creatively and effectively explained what AIDS was, and what it wasn't. She would do it for Billy, and for everyone who, like Billy, was suffering. She would do it for the people who knew them and the people who loved them, and those who neither knew nor loved them but whose understanding would deepen with the truth.

In blue, the colour of truth, the neon MAN sign on the building in front of Dermot, McMasters and Mills flashed on, and she smiled. The answer, like so many answers to life's questions, was literally staring her in the face.

The sound of a car horn pulled her attention to the street below as a battered old Kombi van swerved into a parking space, narrowly avoiding an oncoming car. From the van's sliding door two young men alighted, dressed only in faded flowered board shorts and sandals, impervious to the evening chill. She recognised one as Theresa's son, Miggi, from the corner store and, as happens when you look at someone for no particular reason, he looked up. She waved, he smiled, and his apparent lack of self-consciousness reminded her of who she had once wanted to be.

She walked back into her room and lay on her bed, looking up at the ceiling, smiling and thinking. Gloria was singing loudly next door. Thinking about her new creative challenge made her excited. Thinking about her new friend, who knew about astrology and angels and so many intriguing things she did not yet understand, made her feel warm. There was so much to do, so much to discover, how could she possibly be down at heart? Lying on the bed, alone but not lonely, she drifted into sleep.

CHOOSE

The most powerful person in your world is you. You, and no-one else, can create your future. And though there are times when you feel that events are beyond your control, how you respond to these events is entirely up to you. If you find yourself in a difficult situation it's easy to blame someone else, but it is no-one's fault, it is not even your fault, it is simply a result of the choices you have made – or not made.

If everything you have is a result of the choices you have made in the past, then by the same reasoning, everything you have in the future is a result of the choices and decisions you make now. At all times, in all situations you have a choice. As glaringly obvious as this statement sounds, how often do we stop and really consider what is the wisest thing to do? What is the most intelligent thing to do? How often do we take just a little time to think about the consequences of the choices we make? Of course we think about the big stuff like changing jobs, relationships and moving home. But it's often when we make seemingly insignificant decisions that we behave in the way that we've always behaved, without ever stopping to think, 'No, I'm not going to react like that anymore,' or 'This time, I'm going to do things differently.'

One of the best-loved Buddhist teachers in the west, Thich Nhat Hanh, describes beautifully how the only thing we ever really own are the results of the choices we make: 'My actions are my only true belongings. I cannot escape the consequences of my actions. My actions are the ground upon which I stand.'

We stand or fall by the choices we make, and it's not until we truly understand this and act in the full awareness that everything we do triggers a chain of events that can either harm or benefit ourselves – and others – that we begin to grasp the imperative of making right choices.

There are times to act, and times to think. Always, when you are faced with a decision, do you need to think before you act. This entails thinking clearly about the consequences of whatever action you choose and considering how it will affect you and others. If you lie to someone, what might happen? If you ignore a traffic fine, what will be the result? If you accept an invitation, where might it lead?

Clear thinking and reasoning is a skill that, like all skills, is learned. Yet even when you are confident enough to think in a clear, balanced way and make wise decisions, there are times when you find yourself stuck, unsure what to do.

In times of uncertainty, choose the course of action that will bring the most happiness for you, and those dependent on you. Ask yourself which decision will bring out the best in you and fits with the most perfect vision you have for yourself and your future. Consider how your decision will impact others. Try to be objective and take any negative feelings you may have – fear, hatred, anger, jealousy or greed – out of your decision-making. Think carefully about where your decision will take you, and the people around you. Be honest, and be true to what you feel. If you think no, say 'no'. And if you think yes, say 'yes'. If you say 'yes' when you mean no (or vice versa) you are being dishonest and misleading, and your words will create confusion.

If, after much thought, you still don't know what to do, listen to your body. It is through your body that you can detect your true feelings. How does your body respond to each choice? What happens to your face? Does your jaw soften or harden? Does your body feel calm? Or does it feel uncomfortable? Does it feel sure? Or does it feel doubtful? When you listen to your body you are actually listening to your heart. And though your mind is very clever at spinning you stories that may or may not be true, your heart will never lie. Listen to your heart, and trust your heart. It always speaks the truth.

After you have made your decision, do not procrastinate or postpone taking action. Just do it. If you don't, your mind will begin to play tricks on you and you'll become paralysed with indecision.

When you make your choices in full awareness and you start to live the highest thought you have about yourself, you discover that, very quickly, your life is transformed, and so is your future. You begin to experience firsthand that all that you have is all that you have chosen to create. This realisation is hugely empowering and brings with it an enormous sense of freedom, and also responsibility.

The writer, Neale Donald Walsh calls this 'conscious living' or 'walking in awareness'. As simple as it sounds, it can be one of the hardest things to do. You don't need to look far to see how many people are, every day, making unwise choices and acting in an unconscious, irresponsible way; the politician who chooses to ignore the causes of climate change, the mother who chooses to allow her child to wag school, the teenager who chooses to buy a gun.

It's easy, especially when you are young, to get swept up by something or someone and behave irresponsibly. It takes time – and experience – to learn from a situation and understand how to deal with it better next time. But as you grow older, your sense of individual responsibility grows, too. When you accept responsibility for yourself and your actions, then life becomes a whole lot easier. If you fail to recognise and accept responsibility, you will never be truly happy. You will never grow, or evolve.

Fundamental to the Buddhist teachings is the emphasis on a sense of personal responsibility rather than belief in a creator or god. In an article entitled *20 Ways to Get Good Karma*, The Dalai Lama lists the following advice as one of his instructions for life: 'Follow the 3Rs: Respect for self, Respect for others, Responsibility for your actions.'

You don't need to be spiritually minded to acknowledge the wisdom in taking responsibility for your actions. After all, if you won't take responsibility for yourself, who will? And what is karma after all but the simple, inescapable rule of cause and effect. Yet, though this concept is so simple, we (choose to) rarely even consider it, let alone live by it. In the words of another Buddhist teacher, Sakyong Mipham, 'Like gravity, karma is so basic we often don't even notice it.'

Every physics student knows that it was Albert Einstein who said, 'Every action has an equal and opposite reaction.' Though Einstein was talking about what happens on the physical plane, his theory rings true on all levels. This is the law of cause and effect, the law of karma. And in this sense, it's a natural law that governs each and every living thing. It rains too much and the river floods. The rat eats poison, and it dies. You drive your car into a wall, it gets smashed.

World champion tennis player, Billie Jean King summarised this fundamental law of karma when she said 'Tennis taught me so many lessons in life. One of the things it taught me is that every ball that comes to me, I have to make a decision. I have to accept responsibility for the consequences every time I hit a ball.'

You can, of course, choose not to 'hit the ball' or act, but just as your action creates a consequence, so too does your inaction. There is no way out. You may as well choose the best 'action' and create the best 'reaction', and this means choosing to take full responsibility for your actions.

Some religions take the concept of karma to a

different level in that they preach that whatever you suffer – or are rewarded with – in this life is a result of what you did in a previous life. If this is the case there appears to be very little you can do to affect that kind of karma, so it might be wise to focus not on past or future lives, but this life, this day, this moment, this decision, this choice.

Author, Sol Luckman supports this view entirely when he said: 'Contrary to popular misconception karma has nothing to do with punishment and reward. It exists as part of our holographic universe's binary or dualistic operating system only to teach us responsibility for our creations – and all things we experience are our creations.'

Choose what you do with care, in the knowledge that your every thought, your every decision creates your future. Choose happiness for your heart, choose kindness for others, choose to nurture your sense of responsibility, knowing that when you do so, you set yourself free to follow your dreams.

HEAL

'Real life honestly portrayed is sufficiently dramatic in itself.' She spoke slowly and with eloquence, wasting no words. Seated around the boardroom table with the agency directors, the Federal Government Minister of Health and his deputy listened carefully. 'Real life, real people, real words,' she paused, 'real truth.'

She turned over a large board to reveal a series of striking, graphic black and white photographs of people's faces, 'The father, the daughter, the son, the partner, the grandmother, the friend, the couple, the brother...' each and every one of them tell us, in their words, what AIDS is. And what it is not. They tell us how you can catch it. And how you can't.' The Minister was nodding his approval. She switched on the cassette player and the music to the song *You've Got a Friend* could be heard at just the right volume. She pointed to the first face on the board, 'You cannot catch AIDS from kissing.'

Michael picked up the idea, 'You cannot catch AIDS from mosquitoes.'

They took it in turns, 'You cannot catch AIDS from someone sneezing,' she said.

'You can catch AIDS from having unprotected sex.'

'You don't have to be homosexual to catch AIDS.'

The campaign presentation lasted for less than an hour. Its impact would last for years.

She had reclaimed her crown as the agency golden girl and it felt good, not least because the pride she felt in creating a meaningful educational campaign was far greater than that of any sales campaign. Indeed, feeling pride in her work – and herself – was something she had not experienced in a long time. When you do good things, good things happen to you in return, and it builds a momentum that lifts you higher and higher. She was discovering that the benefits spilled over into all areas of her life, like a multi-faceted crystal that, when touched by sunlight, casts a rainbow of colours around the entire room.

She could have celebrated her success with champagne, or cocaine, or a party. But she was no longer seeking transcendence in ways that led more to pain than pleasure. Instead she went swimming at North Sydney Olympic Pool, moving her body through the water beneath the Harbour Bridge whose graceful giant girders soared above her and marked the triumph of her every lap.

Walking home from the swimming pool she paused on the steep hill to rest and take in the uninterrupted view of the harbour, its little waves jumping in the wind, its jetties devoid of people but not life, and she thought that she would never tire of this sight. For even on cloudy days, Sydney held the promise of the sunshine to come.

Standing alone, gazing across at the world's most beautiful harbour, she breathed in the cool air and thought about the empty home she was returning to. Sometimes, she reflected, the empty times are the best times. Nothingness is nothing more than waiting for the fullness to come. And it always comes. Spring always follows winter. Sunshine always follows rain. Hope always follows despair. And where before her days were dulled by depression and anxiety, now she was starting to see the world around her in glorious technicolour.

Because she was the type of person who, when she made a decision wasted no time in implementing it, she had very quickly embraced her newfound health and, equally fast, was rewarded with a new perspective and calm.

Gloria had recommended a yoga teacher in

whose evening classes she was learning to stretch her body and focus her mind. The stress that she once suffered was evaporating. Now, when she danced alone in her room, it felt better, less frenetic, more defined, though still like a child who moved her body without a conscious thought, but with a wild beauty in time with the music.

She was also making a conscious effort to eat well.

'Where you been? We miss you. Why you so thin? You not eating! You eat. Eat!' Theresa piled a portion of freshly-cooked fava beans with bacon into a takeaway container and thrust it at her.

'Thank you,' she replied, opening her purse.

'No, no!' Theresa vigorously dismissed her attempt to pay, and she was struck by the kindness of people and in particular of this hardworking woman who appeared never to take a day off, and never complained. Not for the first time, Theresa ordered Miggi to come out from the family living room behind the shop where he could be heard playing the guitar, and help carry Jem's shopping up to her room and, as always, he obeyed.

There was something easy about Miggi, something that you might at first overlook; his gentle smile, his deep eyes, his conversation that hid nothing. He was polite but not formal, sensitive but not shy, aware but not self-conscious. He was easy on the eye, too. She observed that he had the longest, most beautiful eyelashes she'd ever seen, like a doll's. At the top of the stairs, he carefully placed her shopping bags down on the floor and almost before she could thank him, he disappeared down the stairs with a wave and a 'no worries.'

'They are a good family, but I don't like her food, it's too bland,' Gloria retorted when Jem offered to share her dinner. They had met, as they often did in the evenings, in Gloria's room to talk, (though it was mostly Gloria who talked and Jem who listened). So she ate all the beans and bacon, and she could feel its nourishment doing her good, and was reminded of something that her mother had told her; that when you create something, anything – a meal, a picture, a flower display – you pour a part of your essence into it. 'Never cook when you're in a bad mood,' her mother had said, 'Good food is love shared.' Sitting in the warmth and golden light of Gloria's room, consuming Theresa's good food and love, she ate in silence, listening to Gloria chattering as she banged against the side of a wok with a spoon and the scent of cumin and chilli filled the air.

'Metatron's the one you need,' Gloria didn't look up from the stove.

'Who?'

'Archangel Metatron. He rules thought. Amongst other things. He helps you focus on what you need to do, inspires you, re-ignites your enthusiasm. Some consider him to be the most supreme of all angels.

'Metatron?'

'S'right.' Gloria returned with a bowl of steaming spicy noodles, 'Now, *this* is dinner!' she said sitting down, and made slurping noises as she ate and talked at the same time.

'Who's he?' Jem looked up at the picture of the angel with the blue cloak, gleaming sword and enormous wings, the same angel that captured her attention the first time she came into the room.

'Michael. Archangel Michael, Saint Michael if you're high church. Warrior, protector, conqueror of dark forces – he's the biggie, the one you call for help if you're in trouble. Archangel Michael, save me, Archangel Michael – help me now!' that sort of thing.'

She snorted at the implausibility of such an instruction but when Gloria shot her a sharp disapproving glare, she quickly tried to sound serious 'Have you ever tried it? Does it work?'

'Of course!' Gloria replied without a flicker of doubt. From the disbelieving look on her friend's face, Gloria could see that an explanation was necessary. 'In spite of the evidence that's all around, and has been for centuries, you cannot scientifically prove that angels exist. Can you imagine if you could? Half the planet would be jumping off tall buildings! No, angels are beings you see or feel or hear or sense in some way. Sometimes they appear as light, or colours, and of course feathers,' she continued slurping her noodles.

'Just like astrology?' questioned Jem.

'Completely different to astrology. Astrology is a science, you can learn it, anybody can learn it. Angels are different. Einstein said as much – not everything that counts can be counted, and not everything that can be counted, counts.'

'I like Michael,' she said gazing up at his image, without realising the significance of her statement.

Swimming strengthened her body. Yoga focussed her mind. Gloria's friendship eased her spirit, and awakened in her a hunger for knowledge of things of another world, things that she had previously dismissed as fantasy. She was beginning to believe that there were many different realities that existed, and how arrogant it was to think otherwise.

Since body, mind and spirit are all interconnected, and since she was starting to take care of her physical health, her consciousness was subtly shifting. Gradually, almost imperceptibly she was becoming whole again, responding more and reacting less. Even her mother remarked, when they spoke on the phone, that her daughter sounded a lot brighter. They talked about the benefits of yoga, a form of exercise that her mother had practised long before it became fashionable.

'Our teacher explains how to meditate but I just can't get it,' she said, 'My mind won't stay still.'

'Keep practising, it takes time,' her mother advised.

Time was something she was discovering, was moving fast. Two years had passed since she had arrived in this land and, with her residency now legalised, she was conscious of time disappearing, not always in experiences she wanted to remember but which made her more determined to make the most of every minute.

Her days were busy writing the AIDS campaign that comprised of television commercials, radio commercials, magazine and newspaper advertisements, leaflets and posters. It · was the biggest and most important collection of work she had ever undertaken.

Her evenings were spent stretching her body, and her mind. Under the tutelage of Gloria she learned about the sun, the moon and the stars, the patterns they weave and how to read those patterns in relation to your life. She learned about mystical beings; angels, elementals and divas and the roles they play in supporting humanity and the earth itself. She learned that the more she learned, the more there was to learn and that she would only ever grasp a small fraction of all the ancient knowledge. She tried to meditate, to focus her mind, to reach the mysterious place of bliss that she had read about, but the harder she tried, the more difficult it became.

With the worst of winter now receding, she made the effort to go out more, to revisit the harbourside bays and coves that she had discovered when she first arrived and explore new ones, including her favourite, Yurulbin Park at Birchgrove.

Sitting under the grey and green gum trees, breathing in their invigorating scent, she looked across the water towards the tiny Cockatoo Island. In this wild place, she felt a soothing balm quiet her mind, and calm her soul. Escaping the streets of the city gave her perspective; the world and her place in it appeared smaller, her problems diminished. Here, she could observe the perfectly poised balance of nature, the light and dark, sun and shade, hot and cold. From nature she was given the answers to many questions, and, gradually, a sense of harmony was restored.

Occasionally, when invited, she would accompany Michael and Sunny on a day trip out of Sydney, north to the Blue Mountains, or west to Berowra Waters. They would stop for lunch wherever they found themselves, a pub or tearoom in which they would bemoan the quality of food and talk and laugh the way good friends do.

Michael and Sunny were planning their life together and, rather than feeling resentful, she found herself no longer aching for something – or someone – that was out of her reach. Besides, she enjoyed their company, their togetherness elevated her own sense of wellbeing and she felt flattered to be included in at least some of their conversations. Would they honeymoon in Bali or New Zealand? Would they choose to live in a city apartment with a million dollar view or an old federation house in the eastern suburbs? Or would they give up city living altogether and go and join Billy in the outback and become real artists? And when would they have children? Sunny wanted a son, 'a mini Michael.' she joked. Michael said he didn't mind what they had, but he wanted to wait until his career was more established which Jem thought odd given that, with no shortage of awards or job offers, they were surely at the peak of their success.

The trio stretched out comfortably by the banks of the Hawkesbury River. A frangipani tree had thrown its scented flowers to the ground and she picked one up, blowing the dirt away from its delicious cream petals.

'Did Michael tell you he's learning to surf?' Sunny asked, with a hint of mischief.

'No. Aren't you a bit old to learn?' she jested, turning to him.

Michael elbowed her in ribs. 'Never too old to learn!' he said indignantly, 'Come and watch, you might learn something.' Blonde and beautiful, not a hair out of place Michael being catapulted around by a surfboard. That would be worth watching, she mused.

It was Sunday and all of Sydney had come out to play. Avalon beach was filling up fast with families celebrating the first hot day of spring. By midday it was thirty Celsius with not even a puff of a breeze.

It was also, she recalled, the day the planet Mercury turned retrograde and confusion reigned. This, she fathomed, was the reason why Michael and Sunny were late and why, when they finally arrived, they were hot and bothered. She sensed that all was not well, and she wished she hadn't come. A voice inside her whispered for her to make an excuse and leave but she thought that would be impolite. So they walked across the sand to the northern end of the beach near the rocks where she and Sunny laid out their things and watched, in amusement, Michael showing off his surfboarding skills, laughing and applauding him each time he stayed upright.

The ocean, she thought, would offer a welcome respite from the rising heat, and she wandered down to the water's edge, and slowly immersed herself in its coolness. Michael soon abandoned his surfboard in favour of body surfing, and with uncharacteristic enthusiasm, insisted on showing her how to do it.

'Go on – you'll love it!' he insisted, and so she followed him into the sea where he patiently explained how to wait for the right wave and, when it came, how to throw herself forward and start swimming towards the shore, allowing the wave to pick her up and carry her onto the sand.

She quickly learned which waves were worth catching and which were not. It was an exhilarating sensation to give her body to the wave, to feel its strength beneath her, holding her, carrying her. She watched how Michael ducked underneath the waves that were crashing above his head to avoid what he called being 'dumped', and she followed his example. 'I can do it!' she screamed, laughing with delight, after another successful attempt at being carried into shore. On the beach, Sunny waved at her, smiling at her friend's delight at this thrilling new discovery.

Life changing moments are etched permanently in our minds. She would always remember how she carefully avoided being dumped by a wave by diving underneath it and how, when she surfaced, she was further out to sea than before. She reached with her toes for the sand beneath her, but there was nothing but the ocean. Undaunted, she started swimming back to the shore but very quickly realised she was making no progress, and the tide was growing stronger.

Her thinking was fast and clear; she knew that she was caught in a riptide, a narrow channel of water that was pulling her straight out to sea and she knew, too, that the only way out of a rip is to swim across it, not against it. And this is what she did. Her weeks of swimming had made her strong and each stroke was aimed deliberately across the current towards calmer water.

She did not know at exactly what point she began to feel afraid. It could have been when what felt like an enormous wave crashed on top of her, pushing her down under the water, or maybe it was immediately after that when she surfaced again and saw that the beach and the rocks were even further away, and she realised her attempts to swim across the rip were useless, and she was rapidly being pulled out to sea.

She could see Sunny in the distance, sitting on the beach looking out towards her and she wondered why, oh God, why could she not see her distress, and she waved. And Sunny waved back. Then she remembered what she had learned – don't wave, keep your arm still, and she raised her arm out of the water and tried to keep it straight and tried in vain to see Michael, and tried to stay afloat and still the waves crashed on top of her. Each time she surfaced, all too briefly, a wave hit her again and pulled her under and back. One time she surfaced and saw how much further she had been dragged out to sea, and she saw two surfers in the distance and she wanted to shout, to wave but before she could lift her arm, another wave crashed on top of her and she was turned, churning around and around, not knowing which way was up or down.

It was then that she felt her mind split in two; one part was frozen, terrified, the other part was completely lucid – she knew she was in danger and she knew she was panicking, but knowing this didn't make it stop, it made her panic even more.

The faster and harder she tried to draw breath, the less air she consumed, the more she panicked, the more she gasped for air, the more she hyperventilated, the faster her breathing spun out of control. With each pull of the waves she felt her strength disappearing, and then she went under again and this time there was no up or down, there was just blackness and cold, so cold, and a deep muffled rumbling sound of water. And the clear – or was it crazy – part of her mind thought that it was funny that it was true what they said about your life flashing in front of you before you drown.

For in the space of just a few seconds, moments suspended in her memory became vivid; she could see herself lying on the grass next to her mother in her garden, she was boarding a plane to Sydney, she was standing on Bondi Beach, smelling the invigorating freshness of the Pacific Ocean, she was walking with Michael, trying not to run, up to the stage to collect her award, she was kissing Pan – burying her face in his long, dark hair. She saw, for a second time, Billy lying on the floor of the boathouse. She felt his bony hand in hers. She witnessed again the hospital room and the machines that helped to keep him alive. Time swept past, the sunny days, the neon nights, her room, Theresa's smiling face, Gloria's angels, Gloria's angels... 'Archangel Michael, help me!' she silently screamed the words, and just when she was at the point where she was falling into the darkness and losing consciousness, she felt something pull her to the surface. Someone's fingers were tightly wrapped around her wrist, an arm around her neck, pulling her out of the darkness and into the light and suddenly she was back in the present, mouth open, gasping for air, eyes open, a flash of orange and white, being pulled onto something hard – a boat? She was trying to breathe but she couldn't get any air in, the brightness of the sky was blinding, it wasn't a boat, it was a surfboard and she was clinging on, being pushed through the water, and she felt a man's hands under her arms and around her chest, dragging her onto the sand.

She lay on the beach, retching and coughing and crying and alive and when she looked up, he was gone.

HEAL

Like a wild animal that retreats from the world to lick its wounds, when you are hurt – physically, emotionally or mentally – you need to stop what you're doing and withdraw from others to focus on your Self.

Where can you go when your mind refuses to rest? When your heart hurts so much it feels like it is physically breaking? When your body is weary, worn out by the world? Take yourself to the silence of the field, to the flow of the river, to the solitude of the mountain. Gradually, almost imperceptibly, you will notice your breathing becomes slower and deeper, your mind calms and your fractured heart begins to mend. This is the healing power of nature and nature's places. By the sea, on the mountain, in the park, nature wraps you up in her magnificent cloak of harmony and brings you back to a place of serenity and perspective.

When you physically move away from your problem, it appears smaller. What before seemed impossible becomes possible, what felt insurmountable is now achievable, what felt like agony is now not quite so painful. In nature, we draw strength, and draw breath for the next round. Indeed, nature reminds us of the 'round' of life, the cyclical patterns that we have no choice but to follow and would be wise to observe; the coming and going of the seasons, the waxing and waning of the moon, the ebb and flow of the tide. Nature shows us that no state lasts forever, that everything comes and goes and comes again, all in a calm, rhythmic fashion. From nature we learn that no problem or crisis is permanent, and knowing this can help us see our problems in a clearer perspective.

In the same way that people affect your being, so too do places. Places of nature are wild places, untamed and free and as such they are sanctuaries for your soul. That's because nature draws you inwards to a place where you can connect with the more gentle and quiet part of yourself, a place usually drowned out by the frenetic noise of your mind, a place you only rarely see but which is always ready to connect with you, and no more so than at the times when you need to heal.

Environmental scientists have a word for the sense of wellbeing we experience when we connect with nature – biophilia. It's a new word for an ancient connection. 'Never does nature say one thing and wisdom another,' wrote the Roman poet,

Juvenal. We can look to nature for many answers, especially those to do with healing.

If you can't get out into nature, you can always bring nature to you. Simply surrounding yourself with plants can improve your health and wellbeing. Whether it's a miniature bonsai or a giant peace lily, having a plant in the room can lower your blood pressure in times of stress, give you some protection against colds and help you feel less tired. Plants have the power to energise and to calm. They cleanse the air and help you breathe more easily, and make you feel happier. That's because plants emit negative ions which have a hugely positive impact on the way you feel physically and mentally. At the same time, they destroy harmful germs, viruses, bacteria and fungi, and so create a healthier environment. A room full of plants is less dry and dusty, and a much more pleasant place to be in.

Nature has so much to teach us if we would but listen. When we follow nature and move with its rhythms, not against them, everything becomes easier. Living in sync with nature is one of the foremost principles of Chinese medicine. Doing the right thing at the right time enables you to literally go with the flow. It's like flying in a plane with a tail wind behind you, making your journey smoother and faster.

Engaging with nature's energy means observing the cycles of the seasons, and the day. It means spending more time outside, breathing in fresh air in the summer months, and in winter, when darkness tightens the daylight hours, withdrawing to the warmth of your home. It means eating more when you need more energy – at the beginning, not the end of the day, and following the rhythm of the day, waking when the sun rises and sleeping not long after it has set.

Indeed, your sleep – or inability to sleep – is always the first indication of how well you are. Plenty of sleep is crucial to the health of your physical, mental, emotional and spiritual self, and if you are suffering from insomnia, it's a warning that something in your life needs urgent attention.

Physically, sleep is vital to maintaining a healthy immune system and boosting cell repair. It is only during sleep that your mind can process the day's thoughts and feelings. That's because sleep refreshes the part of your brain that keeps your emotions stable – one very good reason why it's best not to make important decisions late at night or when you're tired. Studies show there is truth in the notion that if you've got a problem, it's a good idea to sleep on it, as during sleep your mind sifts through the options and by morning the solution is clear. If you need a quick answer, it's best to get an early night rather than stay up late. That's because the most creative part of our sleeping takes place during slow-wave sleep that occurs in the first half of the night.

By the same token, lack of sleep destroys creativity, damages your memory and makes you irritable and bad-tempered.

If you want to induce a good night's sleep, don't read or watch anything violent or upsetting on television, including the news, before bedtime. Avoid eating just before you go to bed – especially fatty foods that can cause heartburn. And whilst it's a good idea to think about a problem before you go to bed to get your creative thinking going, try not to worry about it.

Eastern teachers tell us that a good way to sleep is to lie on your left side with your left hand under the left cheek. This causes you to inhale through the right nostril. They say that if you sleep in this position, you automatically breathe in the solar energies – the aspiring atoms of life.

Sleep is also an effective way to help beat

stress. When you are under stress your body releases adrenalin and cortisol, the hormones that cause your blood vessels to constrict, your metabolism to speed up, your muscles to tense and your heartbeat and blood pressure to increase. Though cortisol is a natural and important part of the body's response to stress, it's vital that the body's relaxation response is also activated so that your body can return to normal. In a high stress job, event or situation what frequently happens is that the body's stress response is switched on so often that it doesn't have a chance to relax and return to normal. At this point, your body goes into a state of chronic stress.

Chronic stress is different to acute stress that induces the 'fright or flight' response. Chronic stress is a physiological state that freezes your body tissue and stays in your body, damaging your immune system, causing you to feel anxious, depressed and physically or emotionally ill.

In many cultures, stress has become such a common illness it's not even considered an illness. Yet it's vital that you protect yourself from the negative impact of chronic stress. Meditation, yoga, Tai Chi, deep breathing exercises, self-hypnosis, stress management and relaxation techniques are all methods that can help you cope with stress. All these practices can halt the production of stress hormones in your body, and replace them with neuropeptides – endorphins that relax tissue and create a sensation of calm, pleasure and wellbeing. Even just thinking about something – or someone – you like can trigger a rush of endorphins and a feeling of happiness.

Though we've heard the expression time and again, there is scientific evidence that Lord Byron was right when he said 'Always laugh when you can, it's cheap medicine.' Laughter releases endorphins in the brain which gives the body a natural high, relieves pain, tones the heart, boosts the immune system and reduces stress. Children laugh around four hundred times a day, yet adults can manage only fifteen. Next time you're feeling low, watch a funny film, play a game, or do something that makes you laugh, and see how effectively it lifts your spirits.

Regular exercise is also a brilliant stress-buster proven to relieve depression and make you happier. After twenty minutes of any type of exercise your bloodstream is flooded with all sorts of feel-good hormones and endorphins that induce a natural high and boost your immune system, protecting you from colds, coughs and other viruses.

One reason why exercise makes you feel so

good is that it helps to get you breathing properly and increases the flow of oxygen or 'prana.' Prana is the ancient Sanskrit word for breath, life, spirit. In Vedantic philosophy prana is the notion of a vital life force comparable to the Chinese concept of Qi, the energy that sustains all living things and which controls all your body's functions – mental, physical and emotional. Without sufficient prana, your mind and body cannot function properly.

Prana is most easily absorbed into the body through the air, which is why your energy and mood are greatly enhanced when you exercise in fresh air and sunshine. With each breath you inhale, you inhale air charged with this dynamic force. Conversely, if you're stuck inside a stuffy room you'll notice how quickly you become moody, depressed and listless.

Yoga is another way to increase your prana, and improve your health and wellbeing. Traditionally an Eastern practice dating back over 5000 years, yoga is now so popular in the West, many companies are sponsoring yoga classes in the recognition that relaxed employees are healthier and more creative.

The word 'yoga' means 'union' of mind, body and spirit, and the practice combines pranayama (breathing techniques) that relax and re-energise, with meditation for improved concentration, and exercise in the form of asanas (postures) that increase strength and flexibility. Because it focuses on the breath, yoga helps you become more focused, more present in all your senses, more tranquil and less stressed.

One of the benefits of yoga is that it gives you a beautiful posture. This can also be achieved by becoming aware of how you sit and stand, remembering to 'align the spine,' to stand straight but relaxed too, shoulders back and loose, feet hip width apart with your weight evenly balanced on both feet. Imagine a cord pulling you up from the base of your spine through the crown of your head. Better posture gives you a better back and makes you look less heavy, and more beautiful.

Since mind, body and spirit are inextricably linked, your exercise time can be a time for mental and spiritual as well as physical renewal. Half an hour a day is more beneficial than a rigorous weekly workout, and is enough to keep you feeling – and looking good.

It is one thing to want to look good, quite another to become overly concerned with your body image. Our rigid definitions of beauty are, sadly, very limited and those whose livelihoods depend on your falling for their idea of beauty and perfection conveniently forget to tell you that changing how you look on the outside frequently makes no difference to how you feel on the inside. You would be so much happier if you aimed, not for perfection but for what is perfect for you.

Take a look at the people whom you believe are beautiful and immediately you see their imperfections. Maybe their nose is a little too long, their forehead a little too high, or their eyes a little too close together. The reality is that nobody is perfect, and things – or people – that are technically perfect are not beautiful, simply because they are not real. It is our imperfections and our flaws that make us beautiful, because they make us human. And it is our humanness that other people are attracted to. Real beauty is not based on perfection. On the contrary, real beauty stems from real imperfection, as captured in Wendy Cope's (beautifully imperfect) poem, *Magnetic:*

> i spell it out on this fridge door
> you are so wonderful
> i even like th way you snor

One thing though that will always be important

in determining how attractive you are, as well as your place in the social order, is cleanliness. In a group of gorillas, the cleanest gorillas are also the most powerful and respected. And, just like animals, we have developed rituals to cleanse and groom ourselves.

Without becoming obsessive, maintaining at least a basic standard of cleanliness is essential for good health and hygiene. Washing your hands regularly helps to stop you catching germs and getting sick. If you suffer from spots, it's especially important you wash your hands often and resist the temptation to touch your face, except to cleanse it with soap and water and nature's own anti-bacterial, anti-fungal, anti-viral medicine, tea tree oil.

When it comes to looking good and eliciting a positive response from people, a winning smile goes a long way. That means looking after your teeth. As well as brushing, do as the Indians and use a tongue cleaner to eliminate toxins and bad breath. And don't forget to floss! Flossing is the only way to remove the harmful debris that lurks between your teeth. Brushing your teeth without flossing is like washing only two thirds of your body.

Eat well. Follow a healthy diet, like the Mediterranean diet that is rich in fish, fruit and vegetables and olive oil. Avoid high-fat and sugary foods as well as processed foods, and limit the amount of meat you eat.

Equally important as caring for your physical health is caring for your emotional health. It's vital when you feel hurt that you receive care and comfort to soothe the pain. The greater the hurt, the more attention you need. If you don't know how to nurture yourself, don't be afraid to ask for comfort from someone else. Sometimes, just having someone to talk to can help you feel better. Talking about your hurt helps you acknowledge your pain, process it and release it. Writer Marianne Williamson says that only when we continue to allow ourselves to feel and surrender our hurt feelings, can they burn away in the 'fire of transformation.'

When you talk about your pain, it gives you a greater understanding of why you feel the way you do, and helps you learn from the experience. It also helps to put things in perspective. In the absence of a trusted friend or family member to talk to, there are different types of professional counsellors who can support you and help you work through emotional problems.

As with most things in life, when it comes to healing and staying healthy, finding the right balance is key. You can sometimes forget to follow the rules for healthy living, just never forget that the best person, in fact the only person who can take the best care of you – is you.

Audrey Hepburn, legendary film star and official spokesperson for the United Nations International Children's Emergency Fund (UNICEF) was frequently asked to share her beauty secrets and often in response, quoted words from Sam Levenson's poem *Time Tested Beauty Tips*:

'For attractive lips, speak words of kindness.

For lovely eyes, seek out the good in people.

For a slim figure, share your food with the hungry.

For beautiful hair, let a child run his or her fingers through it once a day.

For poise, walk with the knowledge that you never walk alone.'

When, a year before her death in 1993, Hepburn was asked if she had any personal beauty secrets besides Levenson's philosophical tips she replied 'If I had them, I'd make a fortune. But I know what helps – health, lots of sleep, lots of fresh air, and a lot of help from Estee Lauder.'

CONNECT

The sky is bigger in Australia, the sea is stronger, the sunsets more sweet, more poignant than any other she had watched. Michael, her angel, had saved her from drowning, of that she was sure. But, typically for a man of dignity, he did not speak of it. 'Gives you a healthy respect for the ocean, an experience like that,' was all he said in a tone that suggested he knew everything about everything.

The ocean was not the only thing she had discovered a new respect for. Prompted by an acute awareness of the fine thread by which each life hangs by and how easily it can be broken, she resolved not to wait any longer to visit Billy at his parents' home in the outback.

'The desert sky at night is like nothing else, boy are you in a for a treat.' Gloria watched her friend pack, 'And this Michael fella, he's going with you?' she continued with a half-raised eyebrow.

'Yup, he's known Billy for ever, and don't give me that look, there's nothing in it.' She paused before whispering to herself, 'Other than he saved my life.'

'Even if he did, it doesn't mean you owe him.'

Gloria's tone of voice was as sharp as her hearing. 'Think about it, after all this time the sun never says to the earth 'You owe me.' Look what happens to a love like that. It lights up the whole world.' Gloria studied the impassive face of her friend and student and, believing her words had fallen on deaf ears, turned to her favourite subject of the stars, 'Look out for Venus, it's low on the horizon right now and bright, really bright – you can't miss it.'

Jem promised to heed her friend's advice as they hugged goodbye. And in excited anticipation of seeing Billy, and Venus and who knows, maybe even angels, she jumped into a waiting taxi and sped off to the airport.

It took her and Michael nearly all day to travel to Mungerannie. The two connecting flights to Birdsville were followed by a gruelling five hour car journey along the Birdsville Track, a corrugated dirt road that connected the top end of Australia to the bottom. The silver tin roofs of a handful of houses quickly gave way to the seemingly uninhabited landscape of the Sturt Stony Desert, in which the emptiness was punctuated only by an occasional twisted bloodwood tree and giant megalithic rock, giving her the impression that they had landed on another planet, or in another age.

The temperature was climbing into the high thirties and under the merciless desert heat she was starting to wilt, 'Why would you live here? There's nothing,' she said crossly, holding onto the seat of their rented four-wheel drive as it bounced along on its bone-jarring journey. Michael, who had visited this place before and who felt at home in its alien landscape, smiled at her bad temper. 'Peace?' he answered questioningly, and looked up at the cobalt blue sky, 'Inspiration? Look, really look, and you'll see there's not nothing. There's everything.'

And as their vehicle dissected the vast terrain she stopped fretting about the heat and the thin layer of dust that had settled on her skin, in her hair, and everywhere, and she started to relax, leaving the city and any expectations she had behind her. As she did so, she noticed a depth to the landscape, and a sense of spirit not at first visible. Michael was right, there was plenty to see if you took the time to look; a flock of grey and pink Major Mitchells swooping on a waterhole, a lone red kangaroo, a saltbush digging in to the desert, parched, refusing to surrender. And where previously she saw only red soil, she now noticed isolated patches of green scrub. Where before the desert palette was limited to the quiet colours of the earth, she now noticed the bright flash of a yellow flowering kapok bush, and an emerald green parakeet in flight. And through the heat haze she caught a glimpse of the kaleidoscope of colours of the myths and legends and dreams of this ancient land, and she sensed that the land itself was conspiring to tell her its stories.

Her eyes and her mind rested on the immense plains that stretched endlessly in all directions, and by the time they reached the Mungerannie Roadhouse she was beginning to find her sense of place in this remote and rugged land.

If the land had existed for millennia the roadhouse was barely of this century. Facing a dirt airstrip, a primitive-looking, single storey timber building sat squarely in front of half a dozen cargo containers that had been creatively converted to guest rooms alongside a portable toilet and shower. The neighbouring property or 'station' was more than two thousand miles away.

Billy and the ever-faithful Red were waiting on the front verandah to greet them. She tried to disguise her shock at seeing him in a wheelchair and the fact that he looked even thinner than before. His neatly ironed clothes were hanging off him, the skin on his face and arms was red and sore. She bent down to hug him and felt his bones against her, 'Welcome to Big Ugly Face,' he said, holding her tight. She pulled back. 'Aboriginal for Mungerannie,' he laughed, but she saw that he had tears in his eyes and she wished, oh she wished that she had come to see him sooner. 'Jeeze, you picked a corker of a day to come,' he spun his wheelchair around to avoid her eye contact, 'someone turned up the oven!'

Mungarannie was teeming with life. A permanent billabong, a waterhole fed by an artisan bore brought swarms of wild birds, lizards and she shuddered to think what other wildlife to an otherwise arid dot on the landscape.

Wildlife flourished, too, in the roadhouse bar with dusty stockmen, drifters and outsiders stopping enroute from north to south or south to north, to refresh themselves with tins of beer; men worn down, like the smooth volcanic stones that carpet the desert floor, burnt red by the cruel and unforgiving climate.

By the billabong, she sat next to Billy on a blanket. A ghost gum shielded them from the sun that to seemed suck the very air from her lungs. His eyes, she thought, carried the shadow of a new emotion. Sadness? Disappointment? He had changed. It was as if, resigned to the inevitable outcome of his illness, he had lost all enthusiasm for living. She raised her hand to stroke his hair, her fingers skimming the scar on his forehead, 'How did you get this?' she asked.

'By not doing as I was told,' he replied and he looked at her and chuckled and she saw, fleetingly, the old Billy, the naughty Billy, and she smiled. 'When I was a nipper, but old enough to read, there was a sign in the playground, a warning *'Do not walk in front of the swings.'* I remember reading it and thinking, nah, I can do it, I can prove the sign wrong, I can walk in front of the swing and not get hit. So I waited until the swing was well back,' he paused, 'I thought I had enough time…'

'And you walked in front of it?'

'Stupid, huh? Apparently I screamed so loud they slapped the anaesthetic on the second we got to hospital.'

She gently touched the thick white scar, 'Does it hurt?'

'No, not anymore. But I can still remember the pain, how it felt.' His hand reached up and covered hers and he moved it to his chest, she leaned towards him and rested her head on his chest, softly, aware that his body ached.

'It's not fair,' she whispered.

'Maybe not,' his voice was, again, flat, 'Maybe it is fair, maybe it's just pot bloody luck or maybe it's just life, I dunno. But I know I can't change it and if I think how unfair it is I'll go mad, so I don't think about it.'

We all carry wounds, she thought. The scar of his wound is on the outside, my wounds are on in the inside. And in recognising his woundedness she evoked her own, and that made her empathise with him in a way she had not before been able to do. She felt a surge of compassion, the thing that makes us human, that distinguishes us from every other living creature. She understood now why Billy took so many drugs, why he tried to cover up his pain, she could feel his pain, his hurt, his suffering. And the deep sorrow that she felt for him merged with her own sorrows, and vanquished dreams.

Compassion brings with it, questions. Questions she could not answer. Is our personality cast at our birth? Was Billy born to break the rules, to push boundaries, to suffer for his individuality? If he had walked in front of that playground swing a split second later would he have avoided it and not been hit and scarred for life? If he had chosen a different lover, or the same lover at a different time, would he not have caught HIV and be dying of AIDS? Is death random or does it wait, decisively, for us at a set time and, no matter what path we take, rises up to meet us.

She picked up a burnt red rock that had lain on the ground for four hundred million years, its smoothness scorched by the sun that would continue to shine for eons more. We might follow our destiny, she thought, we might try to do something good for ourselves and for others, yet this rock, like the land itself, will silently watch our lives and our dreams wither and die.

At nightfall, Billy slept and she and Michael ate their dinner together in the bar, in silence. Tomorrow they would return home. Tonight she would search for Venus.

Burning by day, freezing by night, the desert offers up its extremes, bold-faced for the brave. She wrapped herself in a coat and a blanket and wandered away from the roadhouse, and as her eyes adjusted to the darkness, she gasped at what she saw.

Against night's black sheet, a million white stars stretching to infinity encircled her and spun her around in all directions to see a million more, and more. Giddy, utterly transfixed, she lay on the blanket on the ground and with the earth holding her, whole nebulae and galaxies swirled around her, and around and around they spun, and she felt herself being lifted up and the ground beneath her fell away, and she looked down to the stars below her and she looked up to the stars above and, touching their light, she was joined in the circle of the stars. And she could hear the sound of bells and a lightness filled her spirit, a lightness so exquisite, she could barely breathe. Lost, and found, in the celestial music and heavenly pattern of the universe, she was the universe, and the universe was her.

In the things of nature, nothing could ever compare to this night of stars that carried her breath and all her senses and all of her away. Not even the sound of Michael's footsteps on the desert stones could bring her back to earth. Not even the presence of him lying next her, feeling his warmth against her could steal her gaze.

'Now tell me it's nothing,' he whispered.

'It's everything,' she said, in awe.

And he found her hand and he took it in his and held it tightly, and she turned to him, her face close to his and she looked into his eyes and she saw there what she knew she would see. Light, and love. And a million stars.

Their lips touched, tentatively at first, then more firmly and he pushed against her with an urgency and she felt herself melting into him. And she understood now how we are all connected, how we are all held together, and how everything fits exactly as it should.

It came quietly, the voice inside her, but it came fast. Something, she did not know what, made her pull back from Michael and with no forethought, she spoke the word, the name, 'Sunny.'

He touched her face, 'How can you marry someone when you're in love with someone else?' he said.

She looked at him and she had no answer. She didn't know what to think. How could he not love Sunny? 'Everyone loves Sunny,' she replied in disbelief.

'Everyone doesn't feel what I feel,' he paused. And then, sensing something was broken, not to be immediately repaired, he rolled onto his back and he spoke slowly, 'Yes, everyone loves Sunny. Sunny is sweet, Sunny is kind, Sunny is …Sunny,' he stopped and squeezed her hand, 'But Sunny is not you. And it is you I love.'

She looked at him, unsure, unnerved by his confession. 'How? I mean why?' He laughed, and sighed. His hands, they were beautiful hands, touched her face, and his voice was sure, 'I love you because you are brave, you are beautiful, you are strong, you are wild. Yes, that's what I love most,' he paused, carefully choosing his words, knowing that his future, their future, depended on what he said, or didn't say, 'the wildness of you, your heart, I love the wildness of your heart,' His fingers traced the outline of her lips, and he smiled, 'I love the stupid faces you make when you're writing. I love the sound of your breathing which I can sometimes hear when you are near. I love you because you make mistakes and you are not perfect, but you try, you always try really hard to be better. When I'm not with you, I am thinking about you and counting the hours until we will be together, and when we are together the time goes by too quickly.' He searched her face, 'All of this, it is love. It is how, why I love you.'

She was stunned, and silent. A declaration of love like this was, in itself, incredible. But a declaration of love like this from Michael was inconceivable.

Michael who had the poise of a man who knew himself and who was usually so calm and steady, was speaking as if he were someone else. And then it dawned on her why he was always calm.

He was calm because he'd always done what everyone said. He followed the rules, walked the path that others had paved for him. He was calm because he had resigned himself to his destiny without question. People who dare to break the mould, to tread a different path are the ones who are frequently full of doubt, frustration, even despair at their choices. People, like her, who say 'No, I'm not going to do what pleases you, but what pleases me,' are easily upset, scared and consumed with questioning. And now, here was Michael next to her, behaving in a way he'd never before behaved. Why? Because he was going against the grain, he was doing what he wanted, not what everyone else said he wanted. He was, perhaps for the first time, following his heart. And his heart was telling him that he was in love with her.

She gazed into the heavens, her mind churning, her heart inflamed, and she tried to think clearly about his admission of love, and what it meant. Her pulse was racing. She was excited, of course. It was wonderful. More than wonderful, it made her feel good about herself. More than good, she felt flattered. Then she remembered what she had learned; that flattery is the food of vanity, and vanity is a cloak of illusion that we draw around ourselves to keep out the truth.

'We always have a choice,' she heard her mother's words. She had arrived at a crossroads, a place where she must choose. She and Michael had come together in a way that she had inexplicably always known they would. What if she chose him? What of the consequences? Sunny would be heartbroken but she would survive and no doubt love again. She and Michael would love each other well. They would understand each other because they knew each other. He had seen her at her worst and still he loved her. And a voice came crashing through her mind's logic, a voice so loud and clear, it could not be ignored. 'He is undeniably attractive and there is a connection between you,' the voice said, 'you want him, yes. He is noble and kind and mature and he can offer you a life of peace and security and you need that, yes. He loves you, this is clear. But do you love him?' Again the voice shouted at her, demanding, 'do you love him?'

And the answer came loud and clear. 'No.'

CONNECT

All things are all things to all things. Always, when we reach out to others do we discover something about ourselves. We are not, by nature, solitary animals and it is only by relating to other people that we learn who we are, and grow. In a loud and crowded world it is tempting to dream of living a life of solitude, and though some alone time is essential, too long alone and we become stunted. Disconnected from others, we can become disconnected from ourselves. A hermit existence is for a brave few and, unless it produces something of worth, is of little benefit to ourselves or humanity. If it's enlightenment you seek, you need to engage with the real world. You need to look out before you can look in.

'Inter-dependence,' said the Dalai Lama, 'is a fundamental law of nature.' He went on to say 'Not only higher forms of life but also many of the smallest insects are social beings who, without any religion, law or education, survive by mutual cooperation based on an innate recognition of their interconnectedness.'

Like all other species, without proper interaction,

we crumble and dissolve. Unlike all other species, we have a deep need to belong. We crave the comfort that comes with relating harmoniously to others, we yearn for the happiness that a loving relationship can bring.

The Mayan expression 'I am another of yourself' eloquently summarises the concept of kinship and interconnectedness. Yet, even when we understand that we are all connected and we are all one, most of us fail to acknowledge our 'oneness', let alone incorporate it into our day to day living. If we did, we would not say and do half the things we say and do. We would not be so ready to criticise others, or judge them. If we really felt we were, in essence, all the same, we would think much more carefully before we speak, we would appreciate that appearances can be deceptive and we would understand that we have no idea of who someone else is or where they are at unless we are them, and we would not treat people carelessly because we would know that everyone, everyone, deserves to be treated with respect, kindness and consideration.

'Do not judge your neighbour until you walk two moons in his moccasins,' said the northern Cheyenne. One glance at Native American culture reveals a people who historically respected all kinds of human beings, not judging those who were different in any way. Like most indigenous peoples, they lived in far greater awareness of our interconnectedness with each other, and the earth.

Every society, culture and age has its own method of reaching out and creating a community. Today, many friendships are forged on the internet and social networking sites are the new community centres in which anyone can become 'friends' with anyone and everyone. But until you physically meet someone you have no idea who they really are, or if the connection between you is real. A virtual friend is exactly that – virtual, not the real thing.

On the internet, in the playground or at work, friends come into (and leave) our lives in many different ways. And we can have many friends, but a true friend is someone else. A true friend is someone with whom you feel an affinity the moment you first meet. Someone who you immediately sense inhabits the same world as you, and with whom you share a sense of familiarity and a feeling that you have known each other for a long time. A true friend does not judge you, he or she respects your feelings and can be trusted. A true friend remains loyal throughout all your life – whatever happens – and is a blessing beyond worth. You can lose your home, you can lose your job, you can lose all your belongings, but you will never lose a true friend. And that is why it is more valuable than any material possession.

How can you earn the priceless gift of a true friend? By becoming a true friend. If you want loyalty, be loyal. If you want support, be supportive. If you want respect, show respect. Like all things of value in life, friendships don't just happen, they are made, and they need nurturing if they are to grow.

There are some people who you might call your friends but they are not true friends. They are the people who, when you are with them, and after they have gone, leave you feeling down, depressed or small in some way. They are what are called toxic friends. Toxic friends never praise or encourage you, on the contrary they take a perverse kind of pleasure in your setbacks, and are less than excited in your victories. Oscar Wilde said 'Anyone can sympathise with the sufferings of a friend, but it requires a very fine nature to sympathise with a friend's success.' The Germans have a word for it – people who relish the misfortune of others – *schandenfreude*.

If you have a toxic friend, you would be wise to stop seeing them and spend time instead with friends who make you feel big not small, and better not worse about yourself. You might also ponder on the words of Eleanor Roosevelt who said, 'No-one can make you feel inferior without your consent.'

How do you know if a person is worthy of your friendship? There is one sure way to know if someone is right for you. Ask yourself how you feel when you are with that person and how you feel when you leave their company, immediately and some time later. Do you feel good? Do you feel happier? Do you feel bigger and better about yourself? Or do you feel smaller, flatter and depressed? Do they make you feel cross or misunderstood? Do not ignore your feelings. Always trust your intuition, especially when it comes to other people. People who bring you down do actually bring you down and can cause you harm physically, emotionally or mentally. Of course this is not necessarily their intention and they are probably not malicious but such people can and will sap your energy. When you leave their presence, they feel better and you feel worse.

There may be situations in which you have no choice but to spend time with people who you don't like or who are no good for you. Perhaps you have to work with them. If so, you can protect yourself from their negativity by politely refusing to be drawn into conversations that don't relate to your work and trying (as hard as it might be) to think of their more positive qualities.

The warning here, of course, is not to behave in a poisonous way yourself. Be very careful how you treat others. Do not walk all over their feelings, be honest but be sensitive. If you know that you have hurt someone, say sorry. If you feel you cannot apologise to their face, send a note. You don't need to explain anything if you don't want to, you simply need to say sorry. If you don't, the hurt you caused will follow you around all your life.

Try to be cheerful with everyone you meet. Of course it's easy to smile when you have something to smile about and far more hard when you think you have nothing. But try to smile more often. When you smile at people, you instantly change their thinking and their behaviour, and draw more positive experiences to you. Above all, be kind. Writer and parapsychologist, Aldous Huxley wrote when he was dying, 'It is a bit embarrassing to have been concerned with the human problem all one's life and find at the end that one has no more to offer by way of advice than 'try to be a little kinder.'

As well as being kind in what we say to others, we need to be kind in what we say about others, and that means never gossiping about someone else. Never. When you say harmful words, or even think harmful thoughts, like a boomerang they come flying back to hurt you. Remember the words of Buddha, 'If you propose to speak, always ask yourself – is it true, is it necessary, is it kind?'

Speaking is something that we, as humans, have become very good at. We like the sound of our own voice, it reassures us that we are important, that we count in some way. Yet people who talk all the time, who in conversation say 'I' instead of 'we' are usually insecure and fearful.

We all sometimes choose to speak when we should listen. We forget that we were born with two ears and one tongue, and we need to listen more, much more than we talk. When you stop talking and start listening, you create space for other people to have their say, which is often exactly what you need to hear. Listening also refines your powers of observation and helps you develop sharper judgement. Often, when you choose silence instead of words, you create more respect and a more desirable outcome.

Choosing the right time to speak – and the right words to say – is a skill that we learn as we grow. And though there are times when it is right to complain, most times it is best not to criticise others. Even those you consider your 'enemies' are in your life for a reason. Your enemies, in fact, are your greatest teachers. They bring you lessons that your friends cannot. They enable you to learn tolerance, patience and understanding or some other valuable trait. For how else can you develop these qualities if not by being challenged by someone with opposing views?

If the concept of 'love thy enemy' is a step too far for you, at least try to recognise the message, and the lesson that your enemy brings. When you begin to see your enemy as a fellow human being with human weaknesses, insecurities and fears, you begin to see them as less of an enemy and more of a person.

So often, what we dislike about someone is actually something that is unlikable about ourselves. German novelist, Hermann Hesse described why this is the case when he said, 'If you hate a person, you hate something in him that is part of yourself. What isn't part of ourselves doesn't disturb us.'

You may, for example, complain that a colleague is unfriendly, but if you think about it honestly, you might realise that it is you who is being unfriendly. Nowhere is the idea that 'you get what you give' more true than in our relationships with others.

Almost always, the way you treat others is the way you treat yourself. If you show disdain or hatred for someone, you need to think about the ways you are disdainful or hateful to yourself. Indeed, the most important person you need to connect with is yourself. You are the guardian of your Self, and you need to honour yourself, respect yourself and treat yourself well. Only when you can do this, can you hope to connect to others in a healthy and respectful way.

Taking the time and effort to develop a little humility and appreciation of others people's points of view goes a long way to becoming a happier, more connected person. Think about the happy people you know. What do they share? Most genuinely happy people are not consumed by envy or resentment, they are not depressed or critical or fearful. They are cheerful, full of life and joy. You can see it in their faces. True joy has such a profound beauty that, like a magnet, it attracts people to you.

No-one is more deserving of feeling joy and happiness than you. Nor is anyone responsible for finding your joy, but you. When you begin to relate to others in a positive, uplifting way, something incredible happens. Others begin to respond in a positive, uplifting way. Your enemy is no longer your enemy. The person you thought you hated is not so very different from yourself. And that realisation brings with it a deep sense of unity and joy. You begin to not just see but to feel how we are all connected, how we are all one.

When you experience a true connection with others, empathy and compassion flood into your life and you will never again feel empty, alone and cast adrift on a stormy sea. You discover, too, that there is no end to the thread that ties us to each other and to our environment; the thread that connects us to all living things, to the animals, the trees and all the things that exist that we cannot see. With that kind of connection comes awareness that you are no bigger or smaller than anyone else. You are no greater or lesser a person. It is a beautiful and immensely reassuring feeling that brings with it a sense of belonging and fullness that grows, and grows.

Sometimes we find it easier to connect to animals and to nature than to people. Animals do not judge us, or hurt us. Our pets, like little children, want only to please us. When we reach out and show respect and love for animals we induce a mutual and deep healing. Animals, birds, trees, oceans, mountains and meadows all remind us of the inextricable link between humanity and nature, a bond that can never be broken.

If you have moments, no matter how brief, when you feel at one with others or at one with nature it is because you are at one with others and nature. The more you become conscious of this, the bigger the feeling grows, within you and around you. Gradually you realise you are a part of a pattern that weaves through the world – and beyond. And when you look up on a cloudless night, and gaze at the wonder of the stars above you, you realise that nothing is by chance, everything – every planet, every person – has its place in the order of things, and it is up to us to respect and preserve that order. 'You are a child of the universe, no less than the trees and the stars,' wrote Max Ehrmann in the poem *Desiderata,* 'You have a right to be here. And whether or not it is clear to you, no doubt the universe is unfolding as it should.'

There is no more urgent time to not only embrace the reality that each of us is no less – or more – than the trees and the stars, but to also take seriously the imperative that we must work together to protect our earth, our home.

Relating to and feeling close to the earth and each other requires, paradoxically, an element of detachment or objectivity that can only be attained when you distance yourself slightly. When you stand back you get a bigger and better view.

After spending months in space, Russian cosmonaut, Aleksander Aleksandrov gained an acutely clear perspective on planet earth, and our place in it, and reported what he felt. 'And then it struck me that we are all children of Earth. It does not matter what country you look at. We are all Earth's children, and should treat her as our Mother.'

Mother, father, sister, brother, woman, man, bird, fish, animal, tree, river, ocean, we are all part of the same family and when we truly realise our Oneness, and begin to live a life of inclusiveness, a peace enters our soul, a blessed peace that can never be extinguished.

ENDURE

She had no time to allow herself the luxury of reliving the awakening that she had experienced in the desert. When all she wanted to do was savour the moment, stretch it out to make it last as long as possible, she had to return to Sydney.

Despite being away for just a few days, her telephone answer machine was beeping insistently, signalling that she had three messages; one from her mother's sister, Aunt Eve asking her to call, another from Boss at the agency complaining that he'd had some relative of hers from England on the phone trying to track her down. The last message was from the producer of the film company hired to film her AIDS commercials, enquiring as to when she wanted to reschedule filming.

All three messages signalled one thing. Something was wrong with her mother. And she was catching the next flight to London.

In the stuffy, overheated nursing home, she wrapped her mother's shrunken hand in hers, and squeezed it gently. The nurse brought her a cup of sweet tea, and she thanked her. She was parched, dehydrated from the interminable journey but as much as she wanted to drink her tea she didn't want to let go of her mother's hand, not now, not today, not ever. If she let go, she thought her mother might stop breathing and then it – death – would become real, and she couldn't handle that.

For as long as she could remember, they had held hands. Mother and daughter holding hands on the bus, on their walks to the duck pond, in the Q Fish Bar where they'd meet for Saturday fish and chips lunch. 'My bootiful,' her mother would greet her as she clasped her hand, and she knew that she was just saying that because she was her mother. Every daughter is beautiful in the eyes of her mother.

Now, as part of the inevitable parent child role reversal we are programmed to follow, it was she who clasped her mother's hand, and watched her closely as she closed her eyes. The morphine was taking its heavy toll, killing the pain, yes, but killing too the bright light of life that was her mother. Like the tide, her light was ebbing away, briefly coming back, only to recede again with the next dose of drugs. And the hastening approach of death.

'Marching on,' her mother said brightly when she asked her the results of the hospital scan, 'merrily marching on.' How could she say that? How could she refer to the cancer that was stealing her life as merry? How could she conceive the chaos that was consuming her body as anything but a nightmare? Then again, how could she begin to understand why her mother said the things she said, or what she was feeling? Though the signs of defeat could be recognised in her eyes, her mother would never reveal her fear to her daughter, not when she couldn't even have told her that she was ill.

The daylight dimmed and the sounds and smells of cooking vegetables wafted up the stairs. She stared out of the window at the sky, the colour of lapis lazuli and drifted into a half sleep, and into a past time. She recollected how she used to joke that Margaret Thatcher saved her mother's life.

The Iron Lady was scolding some hapless presenter on daytime television when her mother, unable to bear another word, got up from her armchair, walked over to the television set and changed channels. At that precise moment, a drunken Scotsman was driving his removals van past the house. He lost control of the steering wheel, mounted the kerb and drove the van straight through the front wall and window, smashing into her living room, crushing the armchair, and stopping only inches away from where her mother stood, or rather cowered in the corner.

But that was a long time ago. And no-one, not even Margaret Thatcher could save her mother now. Her mother was dying. Not a quick or painless death but a long, slow death from melanoma; a virulent cancer that was 'marching on' through her fragile body, destroying everything in its path.

She gazed at her mother's face, her sunken cheeks and hollow eyes. She had lost so much weight that her shoulder blades were visible through her t-shirt. Her green eyes no longer sparkled, and her once fashionably cropped hair was thin. But she thought her mother still beautiful, she still made a valiant effort to look her best, to be, what her generation called 'well turned out' with her manicured nails, just pressed clothes, polished shoes and matching handbag. Bootiful.

That evening, she watched helplessly as her mother insisted on undressing herself and getting herself ready for bed. As with a small child, she let her mother put on her nightdress, inside out and back to front, not interfering, just allowing her this little victory, this proof to herself – and her daughter – that she was doing fine.

Only when her mother had drifted out of consciousness, and the morphine had taken her for the night, did she leave the room and the nursing home and return to her mother's house where she and her Aunt Eve were staying, and where she fell into a fitful sleep, waking regularly with a start, unsure what was a dream and what was real.

'She won't eat,' said the kind but firm matron the next morning as she accompanied her up the creaking stairs to her mother's room. 'If she doesn't eat, she will die. Two weeks.' She looked at the matron in shock. For a nurse who was trained to deal with death and for whom it was a part of her everyday life, speaking of death – and dying – was neither a difficult nor taboo subject. But for Jem, who loved her mother deeply, the words were too harsh, the reality too awful to face. Yet, face it she must. Just because you love someone doesn't make them safe. Nobody is safe. A wrong choice of sexual partner, a lorry driving too fast towards you, a faulty gene, a missing molecule along a double helix, a one in three chance of getting cancer, every life is a gift made more precious by its fragility, and a lucky – or unlucky – roll of the dice.

Her mother wouldn't eat because she wasn't

hungry. It was a vicious circle. No hunger, no food, no hunger. Two weeks.

That morning, for a few brief hours, her mother was bright, and they spoke of Australia, and stars, and of being guided by your inner voice. They spoke of many things, the big and the banal, they spoke of heaven, of music, and of calling a plumber to fix the boiler in her mother's house.

'Your father's so proud of you,' her mother said, looking not at her daughter but into space, and she was struck by two things; one that her mother had mentioned her father given they rarely spoke of the man she never knew, the man who had died when she was very young, the man who, like her, had left England to travel the world to make his dream come true – to make his fortune – only to return a year later with plenty of stories of adventures, but no money.

The second point that struck her was that her mother spoke of her father in the present tense, as if he were alive, 'so proud,' her mother repeated, smiling at the wall, before jumping onto the next random thought. Her mother said that she thought the cancer had gone to her brain because she couldn't think straight anymore. Jem tried to explain that it was the drugs, but her mother couldn't understand,

'Can you get these books, darling? Good reviews,' she handed her a list she had written. 'Bonbons,' she said. 'Bonbons, you know those fruity sweets. Fancy them,' she said, licking her lips in anticipation.

'I'll get them,' Jem replied, and left the nursing home, glad to escape the stifling heat and claustrophobia of the room, and the day.

She took the list out of her pocket and tried to read her mother's spidery writing that fell off the edges of the paper. It didn't make sense, '*Nationwide, Pick of the Day, British Legion of Remembrance, Grandstand.*' What she was reading was a list of TV programmes. As difficult as it now was for her mother to write – and think – she had laboriously copied the TV guide instead of the book guide.

It was the first time she cried. It was the first time it hit her that her bright and beautiful mother had gone, and she was never coming back.

Once inside the bookshop, she scoured the shelves for whatever novels by her mother's favourite authors she could find; books by Belva Plane, Anita Brookner and Doris Lessing, all the while knowing her mother would never read them. She then raced across the road to Woolworths where she scanned the Pick 'n' Mix containers for the individually wrapped bonbons, the ones with the little fruit pictures on the wraps. She found them and stuffed a few handfuls into a plastic bag along with some sticky white milk bottles. She remembered her mother liked milk bottles. 'Hyacinths,' she thought aloud. They were her mother's favourite flowers, and they would make her room smell sweet.

A few yards along the high street was Keith's Flower Stall. There is not a huge choice of flowers in England in late November. Apart from pots of the regulatory red Christmas poinsettia and a few bunches of early tulips and daffodils trucked over from The Netherlands, there were some rather tired roses. Hiding behind the roses, were some brown plastic bowls of hyacinths, the tips of their leaves bravely peeping through the mossy soil. 'Have you got any that are open?' she asked Keith.

'Nah, love, put 'em in a warm place and they'll come up beautiful. Just in time for Christmas.'

'Christmas,' she echoed. No, Christmas was no good. Christmas was a month away. Christmas was, might be, too late. She stood staring at the pots of newborn hyacinths, paralysed. Paralysed with what, she was not sure. Indecision? Fear? Grief? Later it would dawn on her that she was having a chairos moment, a moment in time when something unexpected happens that irreversibly changes the course of your life.

Unlike a chronos moment, which is no less significant but is at least predictable as it occurs in the natural chronological order of things, like starting school, taking exams or starting work, a chairos moment is something you cannot plan. Like falling in love. Or out of love. Or being told that you have cancer. For the rest of her life, she would never forget the poignancy of the moment she stood staring at those pots of hyacinths trying to choose one she thought would flower before her mother died. The tragedy of it filled her with an unbearable sadness. The injustice of it made her strong. 'I'll take this one,' she said picking up the pot with the tallest leaves before rushing back to her mother's bedside.

Back in her mother's room, she sat sitting holding her mother's hand, watching her sleep, and she too closed her eyes, and fell into a half sleep. 'Jem,' her mother's voice jolted her awake.

'I'm here, Mum.'

'What would I do without you, my darling, I dread to think...' her mother's voice trailed off and her eyes became blank and she looked at her daughter like a lost little girl, and Jem smiled, but she was choking on her tears, and she turned her head away so her mother could not see her cry.

She had returned home to London to help her mother die because that's what daughters do. And because, apart from her aunt and a handful of friends, there was no-one else in her mother's life. It was more than two years since she had left to travel to Australia, to follow the sun, and her dream of a better life. Two years since her mother had found the strength to let her daughter go, the strength that comes from not only accepting but believing wholeheartedly the truth in the cliché that if you love someone, you set them free.

Back then, it was easy for her to let go of her mother. So why was it so hard now? Did she not believe that death is just another stage in the journey? Not an ending, but a beginning. If she did believe it, then why couldn't she let her mother go with the certainty that they would be together again one day. 'You must drink this, Mum,' she handed her a glass of her milk drink with a straw, the kind of drink that fills you with vitamins and minerals and calories. Her mother looked at it, disgusted. 'Not hungry,' she said determined, pushing it away, almost spilling it. Jem put it on the bedside table and took her mother's hand. 'Is there anything you want?' she asked, and her mother replied, with a momentary clarity of thinking, 'Power of attorney, did you find it?'

She hesitated before telling her the truth, 'I haven't looked for it.'

'Why not, darling? You must. In bureau.' Her mother's speech was becoming was more stunted and slurred with each passing hour.

'Yes,' she replied, meekly.

'Darling, how else will you pay for all…this?' her mother gestured to the room.

'Yes, Mum,' she repeated, not moving.

'Go on, go now, get it,' her mother insisted, as the light in her eyes faded once more.

Years would pass before she would come to appreciate the circumstances that made her grow up, and put other people's needs before her own. Since her return to London, at no time did she think of herself. Perhaps she did not dare. For if she stopped to contemplate her situation, she would almost certainly see that she was being cast adrift, tossed around on a stormy sea, not knowing how to save herself from drowning and, without a lifeboat in sight, not knowing if she would survive.

In the end, her mother's passing was mercifully swift. An extra shot of morphine, a last loud gasp, a slipping away, out of this world, into another.

What can anyone say? What can anyone do? How can any talking help? Nothing can erase the pain of the death of a loved one. Grief is a long journey, 'like riding a horse,' her aunt said as she held her niece close, 'you have to ride it alone, on and on you ride, day after night after day. And then one day, a long time from now, you get off the horse and there will be someone – or something – waiting for you.' And she heard clearly what her aunt was saying. But she was crying too violently to speak.

ENDURE

What life is without sorrow? Who never experiences pain or adversity? And if there is such a person who lives an untroubled existence, blissfully moving from one idyll to the next, is he or she truly happy? Are they strong? A tree that gets blown by the wind grows stronger than a tree that is sheltered.

In the same way that you cannot know up without down, you cannot know happiness without sadness. There is no light without shadow, and the brighter the light, the darker the shadow.

The flip side of pain is joy and unless you are a very small child for whom joy is a natural state of being, you cannot experience true joy without first experiencing pain. Kahil Gibran wrote about the wonder of the nature of pain and joy – two inseparable states of being in his work *The Prophet,* 'And a woman spoke, saying, Tell us of Pain. And he said: Your pain is the breaking of the shell that encloses your understanding. Even as the stone of the fruit must break, that its heart may stand in the sun, so must you know pain. And could you keep your heart in wonder at the daily miracles of your life, your pain would not seem less wondrous than your joy.'

People who know that there is some kind of benefit in their sorrow are those who can endure their pain, and emerge stronger and wiser.

Like the tree buffeted by the wind, when you're struck by tragedy or disaster, you need to dig down deep with your roots and hold on. Just hold on. Gradually, almost imperceptibly the wind will ease, and the holding on is not quite so hard. Talking to others can help. Not talking to others can help. Writing down how you feel can also help. Whatever way you choose to get through your pain is up to you, but get through it you must because there is no alternative.

'If you're going through hell, keep going,' said Winston Churchill. When you face a traumatic or challenging situation, there's only one way through it, and that's through it. You have to stand up, put one foot in front of the other and start walking. Slowly.

It takes courage to take that first step. It takes courage not to crawl under the duvet with a bottle of whiskey and never come out again. It takes courage to face the world. Much is written about courage, perhaps because it is the one human quality that when we need it most – when we're falling apart – we feel it is beyond our reach.

Courage, we think, is the stuff of heroes not

ordinary people. But we are wrong. Courage is exactly what people everywhere, every day find to get through their trials, big and small, and traverse their pain. They endure their pain, they do what *Superman* actor, Christopher Reeve said and what he himself did after suffering a life-changing accident: 'A hero is an ordinary individual who finds the strength to persevere and endure in spite of overwhelming obstacles.'

No pain is more shattering than the loss of a loved one, and few people escape this blow in life. Anyone who has experienced the pain of grief can relate to the words of writer, Mignon McLaughlin when she said 'The only courage that matters is the kind that gets you from one moment to the next.'

No matter how unspeakable your tragedy, you can – and must – find the courage to 'get from one moment to the next.' In the darkness of despair you must move, inch by precious inch, forwards. And though you cannot possibly look too far ahead, you can at some point look back and see how far you've come, and the progress you've made. It helps. With hindsight you can see that somehow, somewhere you are finding the inner strength, determination and courage to face your challenge and move through your pain.

Suffering takes you to a place where you feel you are alone, and although no-one can share in your pain or sorrow, they can extend the hand of friendship and support. In times of anguish when you are shaken to your core, be very gentle with yourself and never think that you are alone, or not being cared for. Know that no matter how bad things are, you are never given more than you can cope with. And though the lesson is hard, it can be learned, though the mountain seems insurmountable, it is not beyond your reach.

Know, too, at some deep level, that this time – no matter how awful it is – will pass. Knowing this will help to steer you through and out the other side.

These are difficult times to believe in, let alone practise the power of positive thinking. But there is one simple affirmation that you can say, aloud or silently, written by Saint Julian of Norwich, a 14th century English mystic: 'All will be well, and all will be well, and all manner of thing will be well.' Whether it's because it's an ancient affirmation that has built up extraordinary energy through the ages, or whether it's because it's expressed the magical three times, or whether it's simply because it touches a chord deep within you, repeating these words can help to draw you out of the darkness and into the light.

Darkness and light. We're back to opposites. Sun and rain. Joy and pain. In your darkest times, the light you glimpse may be fleeting, but it is real. Look for it. You will find it in the kind words of friends, the gentle rush of birds soaring above, the smile of a child. Look for the light. It is the light that leads you out of hurt into healing, the way out of what has gone, into what will be. And though you may feel as if you can never trust anything or anyone ever again, know that you can trust this flickering light. It is the light of hope. And it will show you the way.

If there is any lesson to be learned from our suffering it is perhaps to appreciate the moment, to be truly thankful for the happiness and good times we have. If, then, our happiness – or that which gives us happiness – is taken from us, we have at least the knowledge that we didn't waste the good times, or take them for granted, but that we immersed ourselves completely in our joy, we drank its goodness, tasted its beauty. And though this doesn't make the pain disappear, it does at least stop us tearing ourselves apart, wishing we had behaved differently.

Gratitude can help boost your spirits. When you feel grateful, you feel more positive and hopeful. Think of all the things you are grateful for right now this minute. Perhaps you are grateful to be able to see the frost on the garden turning everything into a fairytale. Maybe you are grateful to hear your baby girl sing. Or perhaps you feel grateful to be reading this in a warm and comfortable home. You don't need to think long or hard to find something to feel grateful for. Every day there is something – or someone – in your life that invites your attention, and wishes only to make you smile.

Be, really be, with that which gives you happiness, breathe in every precious moment and you will find it easier to be with that which hurts. And, just like the tree that bends in the wind, you will come through the storm, stronger.

RELEASE

In the emptiness of the morning that followed her mother's death, a light snow fell on London, turning everything bright and beautiful. She stared out of her bedroom window in her mother's house at the street that, though dusted white, appeared to her to be shrouded in grey. Downstairs, she could hear Aunt Eve on the phone, making 'arrangements'. She knew it was her place, her duty as a daughter to help, yet she was dragged down by a heaviness, a weight that rendered her incapable of even the smallest action. It was as if she were stuck, not moving forward nor sliding back, just stuck in a blank space of empty nothingness.

For as long as she could remember she wanted to believe in life after death. Since her father's untimely death from a heart attack when she was three years old, she had wondered many times if a part of him lived on. But she was far too sceptical and unable to make that leap of faith, and her wishing in some kind of afterlife remained little more than a fantasy. Now, when she asked herself the question, does the personality survive death, her answer was not so clear cut. In life, the personality is constantly evolving, so why would it not continue to evolve after death? Certainly, she thought nothing could be more dull than spending eternity strumming a harp in some place called heaven. Wherever her mother was now – and she felt close – the conventional concept of heaven was far too limiting to be taken seriously.

But it hurt. Thinking about her mother hurt. Not thinking about her hurt. It was a kind of hurt like no other, a sickening, heart-tearing, mind-wrenching hurt that was a constant, and made doing and thinking impossible. And so she tried to think nothing, and say nothing, and do nothing other than stare out of the window at the softly falling snow. And the day slipped away like a mistake.

She thought back to the last time she was with her mother, as she lay dying. 'True,' her mother had gasped, 'meeting, seeing, true, my mother is here, holding hand,' her mother was glad to have expelled these words, to impart to her daughter this vital information. And Jem could see in her mother's eyes that she was already in another world, an invisible world in which her own mother was reaching for her, a world where time past was erased, and all was as it had always been. And in her mother's eyes she saw an incredible beauty and peace, and a letting go.

The solace that she sought, and found, in the crematorium chapel was palpable. Here, in this place that had borne witness to centuries of prayer and ritual, comfort stroked her mind and calmed her soul. The winter sunlight cast its magic glow through the windows, in praise of the divine, and cast a golden light on the simple interior of the space and everything inside it.

Her mother's coffin, covered with a black sheet, greeted her as she entered the church. It was the most confronting sign that death had taken her mother. There was no sign of life. In place of life was silent stillness. Death. She recoiled at the darkness of the thought, no life, no movement. Nothing but an empty body, and it frightened her.

The service was simple and honest. The rabbi spoke of how her mother had 'taught us how to live well, but…' he said, '…she did more than that, she taught us how to die well.' And Jem thought the rabbi's words were no exaggeration. For her mother had died with dignity, never once complaining, always putting others first, kind and giving to the end.

It was her mother's self-sacrificing nature that had enabled Jem to leave England, to travel to the other side of the world in search of a better life. The thought prompted an image of her life in Australia and, with it, the question of when she had lost sight of her dream, when the world and everything in it had become too strong for her, when she had surrendered that which had taken her to a land far from home, that which she swore she would never surrender. And the disquiet within her grew louder, and she knew she could no longer pretend she could not hear it.

After the service, she thanked the rabbi, and because he was a kind man and he could see her anguish, he gave her his time and wisdom.

'I travelled so far to make my dream come true,' she said, 'a dream that seems utterly selfish in the light of my mother's…' she could not say the word 'death', '…passing,' she continued, 'Is that why my dream has not come true?' Her eyes implored him to speak the truth, 'Was it, is it, does God think it too selfish to even dream such a dream?'

The rabbi was silent before he spoke. 'I do not speak of your relationship with God, for no-one can do that, but I do speak of my own experience with God, and I can share this experience with you, and you can take from it whatever guidance you wish. I believe that God is everywhere and in everyone and everything. And, yes, I believe there is a reason for everything. There is a reason for your dreams and your journey and your experiences, and there is a reason why your dream has not materialised, though that reason may not yet be clear. But know that you are not without guidance or help from God in your travels and in your spiritual journey, even if at times you feel alone. Be patient, Jem, have faith and know that you are being guided. Do not try to work out what is best for you, you cannot possibly know what is best for you. Be open, be receptive, and God will reveal your purpose, and you will know it when it presents itself, and it will feel right.'

Because the rabbi was a man of God, he spoke beautifully. But he didn't answer her question, or if he did, she didn't understand his meaning.

That evening, she telephoned Gloria and they spoke long into the night, of death and destiny and dreams. 'I don't know what to do, shall I come back?' she sighed.

And the older woman counselled the younger one, 'Every person who ever had a dream has, at times, given up on their dream, they have been led astray, they had doubted their ability and even the dream itself. But they have never forgotten the dream. And neither must you.'

'It will take a miracle now…' Jem's voice, and mind, trailed off into space.

And her friend replied, 'Not a miracle, just you. Besides,' Gloria continued in a more gentle tone of voice, 'There are no miracles for those who have no faith in them.'

She vowed then that she would find that faith. She would return to Sydney, to her work, to her home, to her friends, and to her dream. And though she wished to let go of the images of her mother dying, she pledged to keep her mother's love alive, no matter how much it hurt.

RELEASE

Sometimes it is better to let go than to hold on. Sometimes it is better to walk away from a battle than stay and fight. Sometimes when you let go, you gain more. And it is not a weak thing to give up, if you are giving up suffering, pain and anger.

It is easier, of course, to give up the little things that no longer serve you well; the extra spoonful of sugar in your tea, the friendship with a colleague who never stops complaining, the daily, mind-dulling TV soap. It is far harder to let go of the bigger things you feel attached to – situations, memories, ideas, habits, relationships, people, even your own pain can feel comfortably familiar and preferable to the unknown. When you've formed a close attachment to something or someone, just the thought of letting go can fill you with fear – fear of loneliness, fear of emptiness, fear of change, fear of the unknown.

Too many times we allow our fear to rule our lives, and the lives of others. Too often we hold tight to that which we should release. Sometimes it is apathy that prevents us from letting go. Sometimes we hold on, believing that we are doing the right thing in the name of love. But is it loving to prevent those you care about the freedom and the life they need to live? You cannot take responsibility for another person's life and happiness and when you try, you make the problem worse. Sometimes, you need to stand back from the situation and honestly examine your motives. When you do so, you may realise that it is not your love, but your fear of change that prevents you from letting go. Fear clings. Love lets go.

Lovers leave, jobs are lost, life is not always good. It is natural to want to avoid the pain that change may bring. But you cannot deny the reality of your situation for long. At some time you have to face it and deal with it, with honesty and with care.

You cannot grow if you cannot let go. You cannot sail your boat into your future if it is still tied to the shore. Sailing into your future, into what writer, John O'Donohue calls 'the springtime of new possibility' demands that you release elements of your past that hold you back. When you let go, you create space for the new to enter.

Just as it is important to let go of situations or relationships that cause you more harm than good, so too must you let go of any anger, resentment and unhelpful attitudes that stop you moving forward. If you think that your negative feelings are caused by someone else, then you have to try to forgive the person or persons who lie at the root of your anger. If you refuse to forgive them for the hurt they have caused you, you will go mad. American advice columnist, Ann Landers sharply pointed out that 'hanging onto resentment is letting someone you despise live rent-free in your head.'

There is no other way to clear your head of a past hurt than to forgive, to give up the grudge, let go and move on.

Do not think though that forgiveness is the same as excusing or pardoning someone. Nor does forgiveness mean that you have to reconcile with that person, or that you have to make an effort to like them, and it certainly doesn't mean that you forget what they have done, not at all. Forgiveness is when you consciously decide to change your thinking – for your benefit and theirs – and let go of any bitterness or hate that is causing you more harm than it is them. When Bill Clinton asked Nelson Mandela about how he felt when he was finally released from his long imprisonment, Mandela described how 'he felt all that anger welling up again' and he said, 'They've already had me for

27 years ... I had to let it go. You do this not for other people but for yourself. If you don't let go it continues to eat at you.'

If you find it too hard to forgive someone, try simply to accept. When you accept that somebody is not trying to intentionally hurt you by behaving in a certain way, then it's easier to look upon them as a separate person, with their own problems. This makes it easier to forgive them.

Once you accept that you cannot change another person, you can only change your own attitude towards them, you take back the power you have handed them and all the anger you felt immediately lifts. The more willing you are to forgive, the more quickly you can recover and move on.

Eastern philosophies teach us of powerful energy points in our bodies called chakras. They describe how the energy between two people is carried to a specific chakra via an invisible – but very real – cord called an etheric cord. The Native Americans believe, too, that the pain of heartbreak you feel at the end of a relationship is caused by the invisible cords of love that you gave to another literally breaking off and rebounding on your heart. Anyone who has ever felt the trauma of heartbreak knows that this is exactly what it feels like.

When negative energy such as resentment, anger or hatred is felt by one person to another, that energy is transmitted along the etheric cord, causing a pain or ache at the point at which it's connected. When you consciously work on forgiving someone, it can help if you visualise a cutting of the 'cord' or thread between you, to physically free yourself from any feeling of pain or general malaise.

Equally important as forgiving others is being able to forgive yourself for a past action. If you have caused harm and you need to apologise, then do so. But don't carry around your mistakes, regrets or feelings of guilt for something that has happened in the past and you cannot change. Life is too short to be distracted by problems over which you have no control. Do not dwell on what has been lost, but what has been won.

Letting go of outworn attitudes, ideas and relationships creates a new and different space for you to enter. Letting go enables you to begin the next chapter in the story of your life, and enter into that adventure with excitement and with a little trepidation, but never fear. There is nothing, absolutely nothing to fear.

The concept that 'nothing belongs to me, everything belongs to the universe' underlies many of the teachings of Vedanta and serves to remind us that the person who has nothing, has everything.

Of course, the ultimate release in life is the release of life. For many people, death is the most frightening release of all.

In western society, we find it hard to consider death as a natural or even sometimes positive event. In our death-defying culture we do not discuss death, it is a taboo subject. Nor, apart from a funeral, do we have any useful traditions or practices to help us recover from the death of a loved one.

Because we fear death, we find it hard to accept it when it occurs and we can, unintentionally of course, make it difficult for someone who is dying and who knows they are dying and who simply wants to let go. How can they do this easily if they are worried about those they leave behind? So often, people choose to die when their loved ones have left them alone. The best thing you can do to help a dying person is to love them and let them go – in peace. Don't make it harder for them – and yourself – than it already is.

Because we're not taught how to deal with death, we choose not to deal with it. We try to ignore the pain, keep ourselves busy and just get on with our lives as a way of getting through it, paying little or no respect to our suffering. We feel too embarrassed to reach out to others, to admit that we feel like giving up and giving in. Instead we keep going, rushing through the next day and the next, hiding our grief and our tears. Yet it is through our tears that we can release our pain, and who could understand this more than Holocaust survivor, Victor E. Frankl who said, 'But there was no need to be ashamed of tears for tears bore witness that a man had the greatest of courage, the courage to suffer.'

200,000 people died today and 200,000 people will die tomorrow. And the day after, and every day after that. One of the world's leading experts on the subject of death, Dr Elisabeth Kübler-Ross summed up our apparent disinterest in this major rite of passage in her book *On Life After Death*, 'Man has existed for forty-seven million years and has been in its present existence, which includes the facet of divinity, for seven million years. Every day people die all over the world. Yet in a society that is able to send a man to the moon and bring him back well and safe, we have never put any effort into the definition of human death. Isn't that peculiar?'

Thankfully, our attitudes towards death are

changing. Books on death and dying are now best sellers. More and more people are realising that it is far healthier – and more healing – not to deny the pain of grief and loss, but to let our emotions wash through us.

This is something that people in Eastern countries do so well; they weep and they wail in public and no-one feels the slightest embarrassment, only compassion. Bereavement is not an injury that can be bound, quickly healed and forgotten. Nor is it one that you ever completely recover from. But what you can do, slowly, is learn to live with your bereavement. In time you can become more aware and understanding and better for having integrated your grief as yet another important experience, another lesson learned.

Death is our ultimate journey and like birth, it is one that we make alone. Plato said, 'The best life is spent preparing for death.' Dying is a part of living, and thinking about death need not be morbid or macabre. On the contrary, it can help you become acutely aware of the joy – and impermanence – of life, and appreciate every moment as a gift and a blessing.

As for the existence of an afterlife, only you

can make your own judgement about whether or not there is life after death. All spiritual traditions believe that death is not the end, but a new beginning.

There are numerous books written on the concept of the afterlife and reincarnation, some more credible than others. But it is not for anyone else to tell you what happens after death because unless that person has died, and come back to life, they know no more than you.

There are, though, more and more people reporting that they have had a near-death experience and a growing number of them are no longer embarrassed to talk about this profound and life-changing experience. Psychologist Carl Jung described his own near-death experience as 'What happens after death is so unspeakably glorious that our imagination and feelings do not suffice to form even an approximate conception of it.'

You must make up your own mind. Or not. In fact it's probably wise that you choose not to 'believe' anything, rather take time, and interest to contemplate the many different beliefs.

In his book *Life After Death,* Deepak Chopra brings together the wisdom of East and West, of science and spirituality to address the fundamental question of what happens to us when we die. He explains how, in the spiritual tradition of Vedanta, the afterlife brings the opportunity for a 'creative leap' and believes it degrading to the human spirit for it to be thought of as confined to simply a body, and a lifetime. 'We are mind and spirit first, and that places our home beyond the stars.'

Tibetan Buddhists describe death as an encounter with a Being of Light who is believed to be pure Consciousness, and our own true nature. Buddhists also believe in reincarnation. But for those who do not believe in rebirth, the Dalai Lama describes different ways to help you deal with your loss in his book *The Art of Happiness,* including 'the best way to keep a memory of that person, the best remembrance, is to see if you can carry on the wishes of that person.'

Just as 'letting go' in life enables us to move into a new space, so it is the same in death. The Native American Duwamish people say 'There is no death, only a change of worlds.'

Hindu sage and Nobel prize winner, Rabindranath Tagore said 'Death is not the extinguishing of the light, but the blowing out of the candle because the dawn has come.'

Christian faiths advocate the existence of heaven as an afterlife, a concept elegantly articulated by

Henry Scott Holland, Canon of St Paul's Cathedral, in his much-loved poem *Death is Nothing At All,* in which he writes as someone who has died as 'I have only slipped away into the next room' and goes on to say 'I am waiting for you, for an interval, somewhere very near, just around the corner.'

Next room, change of worlds, a home beyond the stars – if, when we die, we enter a new dimension and embark on another stage of our journey, it appears to be an adventure not to be afraid of. We can take heart from this and comfort, too.

We can also take solace in the fact that those we love who have died will always live on in our hearts and our minds and, if we choose, in us. They are not gone, not at all. Even the most hardened disbeliever cannot argue that the very least – which is perhaps the very most – significant evidence of their still living is the irrefutable fact that they live on in us. Their love for us, their support, their kindness, their guidance and understanding, indeed everything they gave us when they were alive and that has moulded us into the person we are, continues to accompany us on our own journey. Their love is forever emblazoned on our hearts, their signatures imprinted on our souls. And in this sense, they are a part of us and we are a part of them.

Death has so much to teach us about life. In death, as in life, all that we have is all that we are. And all that we are is all that really matters.

The highest honour we can give our departed loved ones is to cherish all that they were and still are, and to nurture their gift of love and pass it on to others so that they, too, may benefit from their blessings. This is the circle that is life; the circle that cannot be broken, the circle that keeps coming round and round. There are no beginnings, there are no endings. No-one is lost. Nothing is lost.

BE

The birds did not fall from the trees. The sky did not fall. The oceans did not disappear. The moon did rise, the sun did set, the world still turned on its axis. Nothing was changed. Everything was changed. Everything changes with the death of one you love.

Michael was waiting to meet her at the airport. Beautiful, calm, kind Michael, her saviour, her friend. He wrapped his arms around her and she let her stiff and tired body crumble into him.

'Billy?' she looked up at him, urgently seeking an answer. He looked down and closed his eyes, and she knew the answer. And from a place deep inside her, she moaned and from her already red eyes, tears poured and she heaved as she sobbed. And he held her close.

In the days that followed, she did what she had to do and she did her best, no more, no less. She attended meetings, she made decisions, she moved forward, slowly. But she would not or could not apply herself or commit herself to anything that was not necessary. And that included her relationship with Michael.

In spite of her rejection of him, they had grown too close and fond of each other to want to separate and, as is often the case when one person's love for another is unrequited, Michael believed that any relationship with her was better than no relationship. He knew that she needed him, and she wanted him and he figured that, in time, she would realise that she loved him.

'We need to talk,' he shut the door to their office behind him. She remained silent.

'What are we going to do?' he persisted.

It was the word 'we' that stuck. We. Such a tiny word, such big implications.

In her mind, there was no 'we' but she didn't know how to tell him that, or even if she should. 'I don't want to talk right now,' she paused, 'I need time.'

Though it sounded cliché, it was true. She didn't want to talk. She wanted to be silent, she wanted to listen. She wanted to be still, to be alone, she wanted time to assimilate the enormity of events that had taken place, time to mourn, to grieve. Her mother, dead. Billy, dead. Life as she knew it, dead, dead, dead.

At the end of the long day, she arrived home to her room and a note from Gloria inviting her to dinner as well as a handful of letters including a sympathy card on the front of which was a picture of a butterfly resting on a lily, and the words 'You are not alone' with a passage from the Bible that read 'I will not leave you comfortless: I will come to you. John 14:18'. The card was signed by Theresa from the corner store. Also, in the post, was a bulky envelope that bore the postmark Birdsville. It was from Billy's mother.

Dear Jem

You probably know by now that Billy passed away. It was bronci-pnemonea that got him in the end. Thank you for coming up to see him, it made him happy. He liked you a lot. I know because when he talked about you he smiled and there wasn't much our Billy smiled about. I'm guessing you were close. Anyway he asked me to send you this – its his will. He didn't have much material things but he wanted you to have what he did have. I hope your well love, Michael told me your mum died and I'm sorry to hear that. It's a short life, make the most of it.

God bless

Jeannie

With the loss of her son, Jeannie's words were brief. How could they be otherwise? Words cannot describe the indescribable. Attached to the letter was a copy of Billy's will and a business card bearing a solicitor's name and address in Sydney. There was something else in the envelope, something heavy. She tipped the envelope upside down and a key fell into her hand. Tied to the key was a plait made from plastic fishing line. She recognised it immediately. It was the key to Billy's boathouse.

The key to her new home.

Gifts from the gods come in all manner of disguises, though sometimes – usually when you have not the inclination nor the energy to decipher their meaning – they arrive on your doorstep wrapped simply as what they are; a gift, a present of love from one person to another.

'I want an invite to the house-warming,' Gloria ladled her homemade Tom Yum soup into two bowls.

Given the circumstances, Jem thought her friend's request both inappropriate and insensitive but she didn't take offence, she knew that Gloria was not one for niceties or platitudes.

Turning the key in her hand, she thought about

Billy's boathouse (she could not call it her own, not yet), and she recalled the unwavering sense of peace she felt when she was there, 'Now, I have to learn to meditate' she determined, half to herself. She so wanted to achieve the state of nirvana she had read about, but had never been able to reach.

'It's like everything else, you can't force it or it won't happen,' Gloria handed her a spoon and bowl of steaming soup, 'There's no right place or time. Relax with it and it will come.' She paused as she made herself comfortable in her armchair, 'As for this Michael fella, you got to level with him, tell him it's not on.'

Jem knew that what her friend said was right, but she knew too it would be a hard and difficult thing to do.

'Sometimes, actually most times,' Gloria instructed, again reading her mind, 'the easy way is not the right way.'

It was past midnight when she returned to her room. Tired but unable to sleep, she sat on her tiny balcony, staring blindly at the traffic speeding along the expressway and, beyond, the glowing tower blocks of North Sydney. Soon, she mused, she would move to Billy's boathouse and she would trade this view of car headlights for the lights of fireflies, the hum of traffic for the hum of the creatures of the bush, and the flashing neon signs for shooting stars. And just thinking about that and breathing in the cool night air made her relax, and her muscles loosen, and her mind float above the heavy thoughts that crowded her head.

She closed her eyes and whispered aloud, 'Thank you, Billy.' And as she said the words, she felt her body relax and release its tension, and she felt a tingling in her fingers that spread to the palms of her hands. 'Thank you, Mum,' her words came without thinking. The tingling sensation radiated from her hands up her arms, and her heart felt physically warmer, and she felt love pouring into her, and tears pouring out of her as she spoke.

The tingling sensation grew more intense, 'Thank you, Dad.' Tears were streaming down her face but she couldn't stop, nor did she want to, 'Thank you Michael, thank you Gloria, thank you Aunt Eve,' and she breathed deeply and with each inhalation her body came more alive and her mind, too.

Without direction or thought from her, the words of the rabbi came rushing back to her, clear and loud, 'There is a reason for your dream' he had said, 'and a reason why your dream has not materialised, though that reason may not yet be clear.' She remembered he had told her to be patient, to have faith, to know that she was being guided – all these words came back to her and feeling what felt like a pulse, a current coursing through her veins, she felt herself connecting to something bigger than herself but she did not know what. And she remembered how the rabbi had told her not to try to work out what was best for her, but to be still and receptive, and in this moment – the first moment in a long time – that she had found the time and space to be still, she felt herself being lifted by something or someone. And it felt like bliss.

She recalled the rabbi's words that she must 'trust God' and she wondered if God was the presence she was feeling inside her or if it was her spirit, or her soul or if they were the same thing. The word 'soul' came through, and she knew she could trust her soul. Her soul knew everything about her, where she needed to go, and what she needed to do. Her soul had brought her to this place and to this point in time. It was where she was meant to be. There had been no mistakes. If she had chosen a different dream, a different land, she might be in a different town or a different time, but she would be experiencing the same thing. It was her destiny, and she could not change it. There are things that we – our soul – must experience; death, love, loss, and there is nothing we can do can stop them.

She felt that everything was as it should be, everything was right, even the things that felt wrong – the pain, the suffering, the fear – were right. All was right. 'Thank you, my soul,' she said aloud, and almost simultaneously, she felt a wave of peace emanating from a space inside her, a place that was before an empty hole of sadness and loneliness and fear. It was a wonderful feeling.

She did not attempt to, nor even feel the need to explain her experience to anyone. There was no need to explain anything, to do anything, to be anyone. She was content now to just be with whatever – or whoever – came into her life, without always thinking ahead or averting her attention to something else. She was content too to wait, to not approach everything with an urgency as something that had to be got through as quickly as possible.

Most of all she was content to be with nothing, for it was when she was in the space of nothing that everything came into focus, and within a very short time, she found she was thinking more clearly and more precisely than ever before.

Her newly discovered sense of clarity served her well in the days and nights that followed. With production of the government AIDS campaign about to begin in earnest, she faced a heavy workload that would take to her places across the city where she would interview men and women suffering from AIDS, people whose personal tragedies deemed any problems she thought she may have as utterly insignificant.

It was decided that the film crew be kept to a minimum to avoid any further intrusion into people's lives than necessary. Accompanying herself, Michael and the agency producer would be the film director, camera operator, assistant and sound recordist.

What is the unpredictable but a well-disguised plan of action? The night before the first day of filming, a subtropical summer storm swept through Sydney, leaving chaos in its wake. Roofs were ripped off houses, overflowing drains flooded the roads and trees were blown over. Outside the block in which she lived, a huge branch of a Morton Bay fig tree had broken off and fallen on the bonnet of her car, rendering it undriveable. She left, late, in a taxi for the first location and when she finally arrived, the crew were already set up and waiting for her before they started filming. There was no time for introductions. It was only at the end of recording her interview with the young man who had only recently been diagnosed with AIDS that she was able to properly meet the team with whom she would be working for the next few days.

She recognised his face immediately. Dark hair, dark eyes, dark long eyelashes, beautiful eyelashes. His name, though, escaped her. Theresa's son, Portugese, what was his name? 'Miggi?' she looked at him in surprise. He looked up from the camera he was loading into a black case and smiled as he politely extended his hand to shake hers, 'Miguel. How ya going?' he asked in that easy hybrid Latin Australian accent.

'I didn't know you did…' she gestured to the camera.

He smiled, quietly, 'Assistant cameraman, two years now.'

She tried not to appear surprised, but in truth she was. She was also alarmed at her own misjudgement, her own wildly inaccurate preconception that she had formed about him; that just because he was young (though maybe not as young as she had previously imagined) and he played the guitar, and he surfed, and his parents were a hard working immigrant family who owned the corner shop in the street where she lived, that all these factors somehow excluded him from an aspirational and competitive career as a film cameraman. How could she, even subconsciously, make such judgements?

Though the rest of the day's filming proceeded without a hitch and her interviews ran smoothly, she felt inexplicably unnerved by the revelation that Miguel was working with her, even though he seemed not the least bit ruffled by the coincidence.

It was dark when they finished their day's work in Parramatta, an hour's drive west of Sydney. With Michael having already left with the director, she waited patiently for her taxi to arrive.

'Do you want a lift? I'm heading straight home,' Miguel was loading the last cases of lights and equipment into the back of his Kombi van. She thanked him and climbed into the passenger seat, putting her bag of interview tapes on the floor behind her. She felt she owed him if not an apology, at least an explanation, 'I'm sorry if I seem startled earlier, I had no idea.'

'S'okay...why would you? I didn't know you were a copywriter – great gig.'

He drove, through the rain, along the Parramatta

Road, past the unending car dealerships that littered both sides of the road, flanked by the occasional lifeless shop window and brown brick bungalow.

'I'm not...' she wasn't sure why she felt compelled to say what she wanted to say, 'it's... copywriting, it's not what I really want, what I dreamt – dream – of doing, of writing...' she added, clumsily.

'Isn't it?' he asked, and asked no more. And she didn't volunteer any more information. They talked instead about the day, the people they had met, the work they were doing, the importance of the message they were trying to communicate, they talked about last night's storm and the damage it caused. He was easy to talk to, she liked the way he said not too much, nor too little. They talked the whole journey home.

He pulled up outside the entrance to the building in which she lived, a few doors down from his parents' store, and switched off the engine. She sat still, perhaps a moment too long, before reaching behind her seat to retrieve the bag of interview tapes.

'Here,' he switched on a light inside the van making it easier for her to see.

And what she saw stopped her in her tracks.

A white surfboard was on the floor of the van.

A white surfboard with a flash of orange.

As she stared at it, she saw it, again, in the water, she remembered its hard surface, she remembered her fingers gripping its edges, never letting go. She was transfixed, unable to take her eyes off the surfboard. Was she wrong? No, she wasn't wrong, she knew it.

She looked at him, and he looked at her, and neither of them looked away. The two of them sat looking at each other for what seemed an eternity. 'It was you,' she said, quietly, in disbelief.

'It was me,' he replied.

She raised her hand to her mouth. All this time, she had believed it was Michael who had rescued her from drowning. She was stunned, her mind was racing. In an instant, everything fell into place. Michael. Miguel. Same name. Different language.

Same angel.

And, for the second time that day, she wondered how she could have been so presumptuous, so short sighted not to be able to see things for what they really are, instead of what she imagined them to be.

She recollected what Gloria had told her about Archangel Michael, and one of the ways in which he works. His sword is sharp and swift, it cuts through the veil of illusion and all that is false, so that truth can flow forth, and free. How could she not have recognised the truth? Then again, how could she? She felt confused, and small. And, strangely, excited.

BE

We live in a fast world that's getting faster by the minute. Talk to any elderly person and they will tell you that the older you get, the faster time flies. Yet this 'quickening' phenomena is now affecting younger people, too. Busy, busy, busy, how busy are we? The more so-called labour-saving devices we invent, the more labour we find to do. The faster our computers run, the more work is piled on our desks. The more television channels we are given, the less time we find to sit down and watch them. We have become so busy doing, working, wanting, getting that we have little or no time for being. Just being.

Then there is the noise. Our world has become an increasingly noisy place to be. And though music can be uplifting and some primordial sounds are even proved to heal, the general cacophony of sounds that surrounds us grows every day louder and more intrusive, fighting for our attention – the television, the radio, the commercials that are played in every shop and every building, the automated voice commentary on the bus ride home, the traffic, the mobile phones that have become welded to our bodies and which we cannot go anywhere without.

All these sounds crowd our mind, confuse our thoughts, and add to the sensation that we are being swept along on a turbulent tide of activity from which we cannot escape.

The natural remedy to noise is peace. It is only when the noise ceases and all becomes silent that your mind can calm. And it is only when your mind is calm that you can properly process your feelings, thoughts and ideas. In reply to the question 'What are the fruits of silence?' Ohiyesa (Dr. Charles Eastman) of the Santee Sioux said that he – the American Indian – will say 'They are self-control, true courage or endurance, patience, dignity, and reverence. Silence is the cornerstone of character.'

If we follow the rhythms of nature, night is our quiet time, the time when we can slow down and cast our minds over the day's events, and plan for the next. But no matter what time of day, time spent alone in your own personal space is time richly rewarded.

We give so much of our time, but how often do we take time? Time to be alone, to sit and do nothing, to reconnect with a part of ourselves, our inner voice that we have forgotten but which never forgets us, and always knows what is right for us. Far from a waste of time, time spent alone in silence and stillness can help you get in touch with all the different parts of you. It helps you see things more clearly, solve problems, rediscover what is really important, and who you really are. Time spent alone is the fastest, most effective way to re-energise and renew your Self.

If you're feeling confused, anxious and overstretched, it's a sign that you need to stop doing, and start being. When you take the time to simply be, you take time to nourish your Self. In his book *Stillness Speaks,* Eckhart Tolle writes extensively about the profound wisdom and understanding that is gained by embracing silence and stillness, 'When you lose touch with inner stillness, you lose touch with yourself. When you lose touch with yourself, you lose yourself in the world.'

A lot has been written about the importance of living and being in the present – the now – and for good reason. The present is the only moment that exists. The past has gone and you cannot change it, and if you live in the past you miss out on all the opportunities that are here. Similarly, the future doesn't exist and it's futile to spend all your time daydreaming about it. All that happens, all that is real, is happening now. The present is the only reality, it is the only place where you are, and where all time – and all things – are joined. The present moment holds everything you have become, and everything you need to know.

When you are living in the moment, even in the most mundane situations, you discover that you're in a completely natural state of being and, because it's natural, everything immediately becomes easier; your doing becomes almost effortless as you're more relaxed and find yourself going with the flow. When you're in the moment, you are less disturbed by situations or events around you, your thinking becomes sharper and more creative, and the choices you make, infinitely wiser.

As with all things, nature has much to teach us about the power of living in the moment. It is, after all, the only way that animals live. Animals don't think about tomorrow or next week, all they think about is now – food, rest, shelter and warmth. As a result, they possess extraordinary intuition and presence. Some people too have this special quality. If they seem less stressed and more tuned-in it's because they are.

It is not difficult to reconnect with your real Self, to discover the voice within you, the voice of your soul, and to change the quality of your life. All it takes is a little time and space in which you can switch off your phone, sit down, relax and look at the world around you. If you can do this close to nature, in a park or by the water, so much the better. But wherever you choose to stop and sit, do just that – just sit silently and observe what is happening. Your mind will no doubt want to make judgements and pass commentary on what you see but try to let these thoughts go and simply look, listen and feel what is going on immediately around you.

Look at the sky, breathe in the air, see the birds, the insects, the leaves on the trees, the dew on the grass, smell the wood fire burning, hear the sound of the water tumbling over stones, the bird calling, the dog barking in the distance. Savour the moment for as long as you can. Gradually, your mind will come into focus, your heartbeat will slow, and your breathing will deepen. When you are ready – it may be fifteen minutes or an hour – you can rejoin the rest of the world, relaxed and refreshed.

If you spend quiet, me-time alone each day, you will very quickly notice that you feel more serene and calm, and you see the world and everything in it in a new light, one that is far richer, more respectful and true.

The 17th century philosopher, Blaise Pascal said, 'All men's miseries derive from not being able to sit in a quiet room alone.' It is a belief echoed by many writers and philosophers, past and present, including Nietzsche who said, 'Our greatest experiences are our quietest moments.'

When we are quiet, we come back to ourselves. When we are still, we know.

Being still, being in the moment is a form of meditation. In this sense, you can be meditating in any activity in which your mind and body is totally immersed, be it walking through a forest, ironing a shirt, or building a model car. If you think meditation is something mystical or religious and far removed from normality, think again. Along with its rise in popularity comes a mountain of scientific research that shows that regular meditation triggers a relaxation response which includes lasting changes in metabolism, heart rate, blood pressure and brain chemistry, and which can help with a whole range of medical conditions associated with stress.

In 2008, the National Academies of Sciences published a report that concluded that 'the effects of meditation are widespread and profound. Practitioners report such varied effects as increased attention and memory, improved heath, decreased feelings of stress, and better ability to handle difficult people and situations. Importantly, many of the reported effects occur not during the period of meditation, but rather throughout the day.'

The study reported that results from MRI scans of the brains of people who meditated revealed long-lasting changes in several brain regions involving attention, memory and emotions, and that meditators are better at integrating their thoughts and emotions, and making faster, more skilful decisions.

Scans also revealed that because meditators have more grey matter in their frontal lobes – the part of the brain associated with ageing, meditation can actually slow down the ageing process. Meditation also increases levels of the youth hormone, and magic formula for energy, DHEA, which is why people who regularly meditate look younger.

In addition, the natural high that meditators talk about is supported by the fact that meditation releases higher levels of serotonin, the feel-good chemical in the brain and the same chemical that is released by the drug ecstasy and imitated by LSD. Little wonder then that some people who meditate describe it as pure bliss!

Some call it bliss. Others call it ecstasy. The mystic, Thomas Merton called it a place of pure light. They are all good descriptions. The Tibetan monks call it your Atman, your eternal Spirit. In his book *The Gentle Art of Blessing*, Pierre Pradervand writes, 'Deep inside you exists a space of infinite beauty and rest, of dancing joy and playful being, or limitless vision and infinite abundance. This space constitutes our true being.' Pradervand is describing the spirit, which many believe to be the meditative place.

Whatever you choose to call it, however you describe it, the place of meditation induces the most incredible sensations, empowering yet peaceful, calming yet strengthening. And though some drugs can take you to this place, getting there through meditation is infinitely better than any drug. It's free, it's legal, it's healthy, and the only after effects are positive ones.

One other similarity between drugs and meditation is that both are addictive. Once you've reached this place through meditation, you will want to return, again and again. And, unlike taking drugs, the more you meditate, the stronger the sensation. You cannot develop a tolerance to meditation. Unlike drugs, you don't need to increase the dose to achieve the same effect. Each and every time you meditate (with a few exceptions) you will find it easier and faster to reach that 'high' than the last time. You will, with practice, be able to touch the very essence of you, the place that, when everything around you is changing, remains constant and steady. Meditation will take you to this core. But, like any place you've never been to before, you need directions on how to get there.

Most spiritual traditions teach some form of meditation, and they all involve turning your attention away from the outside world to look within, and quieting the mind to focus on the present moment.

Telling your mind to shut up can be hard, and even harder at the end of a busy day when your mind wants to consider every piece of information it has digested. That's why many people prefer to meditate first thing in the morning. The mind is a powerful tool, and it seems that the more trivial the thought, the more persistently it knocks at your mind's door. 'Hey, don't forget to go to the bank.' Or 'Shouldn't you be working on that assignment?' How do you stop this incessant chatter that the Hindus call your 'monkey mind?'

The trick is to focus on your breathing. This is the best way to start. Set aside twenty minutes when you can sit in a quiet place where you won't be disturbed, and in a comfortable position with your spine straight, your hands resting in your lap or on your knees, palms and fingertips softly pointing upwards. Your hands are powerful energy centres and by turning them upwards you will be able to draw energy to you. For even greater effect, have your thumbs touch your forefingers. This is a well known mudra, or hand posture that keeps the energy circulating around your body. If you feel tension in any part of your body, you can release the tension by scrunching up those muscles, then letting them go.

Become aware of your breathing, don't try to change it, just be aware of how you are breathing. If you can, close your mouth and breathe through your nose. With each inhalation, feel the cool air coming in and with each exhalation feel the warm air leaving the nostrils. Try to focus only on your breathing. When a thought invades (which it surely will), don't engage in the thought but let it go and bring your mind back to your breathing. Feel your breath come in through your nostrils, pass down your throat and into your chest. By focussing on your breath, you will be able to still your mind.

Another way to still your mind and quell those racing thoughts is to repeat a mantra, that is a few words or a phrase that feels good to you and that you can say aloud or silently to yourself. All traditions have a mantra meditation technique. 'Om' (pronounced A-U-M) is a sacred word and Hindu mantra that is thought to be the primal sound of the universe. It has a certain tone that, with concentration, you can feel vibrating through your body. If that feels too esoteric, try something as simple as 'Let love and light fill me with peace.' Or, something even less ethereal and more simple, 'Peace.'

The point is it doesn't matter what you say, only that you say something, and that you really focus on it as you keep repeating it. When you say the words and think about the words, it becomes hard to think about anything else. Repeat your mantra ten or twenty times or as many times as it takes for you to feel relaxed. If and when your mind begins to wander, simply come back to your mantra.

As well as or instead of a mantra, you can choose to focus on an image that you like. It could be a beautiful ocean, a garden or the gentle flame of a candle. You might prefer to visualise a sun or a star above your head radiating its warm light through you. Another lovely sensation can be felt by simply imagining your favourite colour, first in your forehead, then flooding through your whole body. Visualisation can be a very effective way to still your mind, and put aside your busy thoughts.

For many beginners this is the hardest part – actually being able to let go of their thoughts and emotions. Some people find it difficult to even sit still, let alone 'think' still. Sometimes the harder you try, the harder it seems to become. If you feel like you're making no progress, don't get disheartened. Take it a step at a time, it can take days, weeks or even months of practice before you notice any changes.

Meditation is a skill and like any skill, it takes time – and repetition – to learn. The more you practise, the better you get.

As with many things in life, often the moment you stop trying to make it happen, it happens. In a moment of relaxation, you may begin to feel a subtle but very real shift taking place.

Often, the first sign that you're moving in the right direction is that you feel a tingling in your fingers or the palms of your hands. Gradually, you notice your body feels heavy as it is dropping and letting go, and waves of deep relaxation wash over you. Then, as the jabbering voices in your mind fade, you enter your own sacred space.

No-one can tell you what your sacred space

will look or feel like, but trust that you will know when you are there. You will feel a deep sense of calm combined with excitement at having arrived at a place of indescribable peace and joy. A place in which the world around you falls away, all the stresses of your life disappear and an exquisite sense of stillness permeates your whole being. A place that feels like home.

Stay in your sacred space for up to twenty minutes. Do what you want with its power. Use it to affirm what you want to do, or who you want to be. Or give thanks for all the wonderful things in your life and feel your appreciation growing. Or just think of nothing in particular and let that 'nothing' take you wherever it wants to go, a trip into the unknown, and enjoy simply deep breathing in and out what can be described as pure beauty.

When you are still, when you engage with your real Self, you realise, perhaps for the first time, that you are complete, and everything becomes clear. There is no place to go, there is nothing to do, everything you need you have in this wondrous moment.

You will discover what so many people today have lost touch with or are too busy to contemplate, unaware that if they did so, it would make the busy calm, and the calm ripe with potential. The ancients knew all about the power of connecting to your essence. The Chinese philosopher, Lao-Tzu was well aware of how it can transform your life when he said, 'The way to use life is to do nothing through acting, the way to use life is to do everything through being.'

You don't need to shut yourself off from the world to meditate. Once you discover that beautiful, calm space within yourself, you can, in time, choose to go there when you're in the middle of doing anything (well, almost anything). Sitting on the bus, preparing a meal, or doing your chores.

If you can find that sense of calm in any place, if you can call on it at will, and if you discover for yourself that your mind, your emotions and your thoughts are not the real you, then nothing and no-one in this world can ever really hurt you.

'Close my eyes so I can see,' sang REM's Michel Stipes. Maybe he knew something about the power of taking the time to simply be, and using that time to meditate on what you want. If so, it would certainly explain the next line of the song: 'Make my make-believe, believe in me.'

When you close your eyes, even briefly, and bring your attention to your inner Self, you gather together all the wisdom that is stored in your soul. Can you imagine being able to access all that soul wisdom? What dreams will you manifest? What 'make-believe' will you make come true?

LOVE

He came to her when the moon was new, an auspicious start to any relationship. What celestial connection is at work? she wondered. And when did their relationship really begin? Perhaps it was the day he carried her shopping home. Every fibre of his being had wanted to be close to her, but he was shy and when she paused, expectantly, at her door, waiting for him to say something, he ran off. Maybe it began the first time he saw her, in his parents' shop. He was struck by her beauty, so struck that he almost knocked her over with his surfboard. Ah, his surfboard, his trusty white steed that, in the fairytale that was their love, would rescue her from certain death.

Would they live happily ever after? Heaven only knows. And, of course, heaven did know. But it wasn't about to reveal all its secrets, not all at once.

Inside the boathouse, dust had settled on every surface. When you're discovering love, things like dust no longer matter. Boxes of her belongings piled on top of each other, waiting to be unpacked. The boxes could wait.

He had brought food to eat and wine to drink. Something stirred in her as she watched him, a recognition of someone, a soul, she had known a long time, and she felt a sense of familiarity and a lightness, and a joy so quick and uplifting. She could see too that his apparent ease belied a deep dignity and a quietness that she found immensely comforting. On the balcony overlooking the still, warm water, they sat and ate together and talked, as if they had sat and talked all their lives. And he revealed to her his dream.

Ever since he could remember, he had dreamed of making a film, a film in which he created images that were as powerful as the message. And she wept, silently, at the synchronicity of their dreams, of how their lives and their futures were intertwined before they had even met. His dream, like hers, had formed when he was young, it had called him forward to a place that gave meaning to his life, and a purpose for living.

He is like me, she thought.

He is not like me, she thought. He is following his dream, he has not sacrificed his dream for the sake of a job, an income, for something else that is far removed from where or what or who he wants to be. He is calm and focussed, not like me, tossed around on the sea of life.

She knew then that she loved him, and at that point she needed nothing in return, not even the knowledge that he loved her, too.

'What do you want to do?' Miguel handed her a glass of chilled wine that she sipped slowly, enjoying the way it cooled her lips and made them taste sweet. She looked at him, in silence. He ventured, 'You said, coming home from the shoot last week that you didn't really want to be a copywriter. So what do you want to be...do?'

She thought carefully before she spoke, 'I don't know if you'd believe me if I told you.'

'I'd believe you,' he said simply.

She gazed across the water, and she decided she could trust him with her dream. And so she found the courage to speak her truth, to tell him of her dream that led her to this place, the dream that had always been in the background of her life, the dream that matched his own.

She spoke of wanting to write a film, an important and powerful film that would make a difference to people's lives. She spoke of the place in which she dreamed she would write, on an old pine table in a rundown, wooden house by the water and as soon she spoke the words, the words fell into their logical place, and she stopped speaking and she stared at him, silenced by the realisation and the profundity of what she had said.

'And the dream came true,' he finished her sentence, and he laughed as she sat frowning at him.

'I never thought of it like that,' was all she could say.

'Your AIDS campaign. And this,' he gestured to the boathouse.

'The house by the water,' she smiled.

'The wooden house by the water,' he corrected her, 'My mother always says be careful what you wish for.' And this time it was her turn to laugh at the thought of Theresa whose everyday advice was so commonplace that she took little notice of it and did not recognise it as the truth. But it was the truth.

There was a short silence as the space, the very air between them absorbed the significance of the revelation and the truth tumbled down into place.

The truth had always been there, even if she hadn't recognised it. She had followed her dream, and her destiny.

She had written a film, albeit not a long film,

but the importance of which was immeasurable.

She was living in a wooden house by the water, though that too had manifest in a way she could not possibly have predicted.

And what of the most important thing of all, what of love? Love, too, was always there, right under her nose, if she had just stood still for long enough to let love find her, instead of always searching, running into the distance.

She wanted then to tell him that she had dreamed of meeting a man like him, a noble man who would love her as much as she loved him. But, she thought, that would be too much for one day.

Every Sunday for a month, he came to visit her, always with a gift, sometimes he brought food – delicious pastries made with honey or a box of ripe mangoes or fresh figs. Sometimes he bought wine, or flowers – and a crystal vase in which to display them. One time, he brought her a book of poetry he thought she might like.

Some days, he brought his guitar and he would strum the songs of Bob Dylan or The Beatles, but she preferred it when he played a traditional Fado, a melancholic melody from the land of his ancestors, to which she would dance, not a wild dance but a slow, dreamy dance that matched the haunting rhythm of his music.

Another time he arrived – to her amazement – with a boat. 'You can't live in a boathouse without a boat' he declared as he untied the tiny but beautiful old wooden sailing boat from the roof of his Kombi. Together they carried the boat down to the water, and she squealed with laughter when she stepped in and nearly tipped it over.

The afternoon was spent in splendid isolation, bobbing up and down in the boat on Pittwater, catching fish for their supper, enjoying the warmth of the sun, and the easy conversation that flowed between them.

Together they explored the story of each other's history and, at the same time, they began to create their own. There was no script written of where they were going, not even a map of the stars to point the way. They were guided by their hearts, and they trusted their hearts.

One Saturday he arrived at dusk, unannounced. He had been surfing at Whale Beach and he could not wait another day to see her. He did not talk. He touched her face, and his touch made her belly burn with desire. She leaned towards him, and he kissed the graceful arc of her neck, and their mouths met and they found each other, and the borders of their reality dissolved. He tasted of the sea. This she would always remember, the taste of the sea on his skin.

When she looked into his eyes, she sensed that he knew all her thoughts, all her feelings, all her past, her pain and her peace. Peace. Afterwards, lying in his arms, wrapped in his calm, she found a place of peace, of shelter, a place that made her feel safe.

Love. It is the only thing that matters because it is the only thing that is real, she mused, as she sat on the balcony gazing at the reflection of the sliver of the moon in the dark water. She felt too alive to sleep. Material things are not real, money is not real, she thought. Only love is real. And because love is real, love never dies. Not even with death. And she thought of her mother, and Billy and she wondered if it was wrong to feel such happiness when she was still mourning their loss. And as she thought of them she sensed the nearness of them and felt their love pouring into her heart, and she knew without doubt that they too were happy at the joy she felt, and the peace she had found, and the love that had set her free.

She turned to look at Miguel through the open door, sleeping, oblivious to her gaze, and the night swam swiftly away like a fish in the water.

LOVE

To love and to be loved, it is said, is the only true happiness in life. Our need for love lies at the very foundation of human existence, and is true for all people, everywhere. 'Love and compassion are necessities, not luxuries,' said the Dalai Lama, 'Without them humanity cannot survive.'

Of course, there are different kinds of love. The love you feel for a parent, a child or a friend is different to the love you feel for a partner. And even the love you feel for a partner has different stages, each producing its own emotional, physical and mental response – all of which play a vital part in the way we reproduce, and indeed the survival of the human race. From physical and romantic desire to lasting attachment, the love we yearn for is a universal experience to which our brains are inextricably wired.

Science aside, nothing comes close to the power of love. For there is nothing on this earth about which so much has been written, sung, painted, created, longed for, fought over, won and lost than love. Nor is there any other feeling capable of producing such strength of emotion, ecstasy, pain and suffering.

With love, we come alive and so, too, does the world. With love, we feel complete, and can happily live without other things. Without love, we can have all the things in the world and still not be happy.

If it is our nature to want to love and be loved, why then do we find it so hard? Is it that we want it too much? Or is it that we no longer live by a set of principles in which love between two people can be nurtured and grow? Or is the opposite in fact true? Do we now impose upon ourselves a set of impossible criteria that limits us and prevents us ever finding love and happiness?

Perhaps, before you can expect to love someone and be loved in return, you need to learn to love yourself. After all, if you don't love yourself, how can you expect someone else to? If you don't take the time to explore who you really are, how can you possibly know what – or who – you want to share your life with? If you can be alone and be happy, and not hand the reins of your happiness to someone else, you are far better able to develop a loving and longer lasting relationship.

To understand the real you, you need to ask yourself questions, and be honest in your answers. Do you think you'd make a good partner? Why? Are you are secure, emotionally and financially? If not, what can you do to improve that? Do you have problems trusting people? If so, you need to resolve those problems. Can you communicate well? Or do you need to learn how to get on better with people in general? Are you happy with yourself? Your first relationship has to be with yourself, and that means getting to know yourself, and feeling genuinely happy with who you are. When you feel good about yourself, others also feel good about you and want to be around you. When you know who you are, you can then work out what you want in a relationship.

What things are important to you? It might help if you write them down. Is fidelity important to you? Do you need time alone? How much time alone? Do you want to take separate holidays? What about children?

Finding love is not so very different from finding anything else you want in life. You need to know what it is you're looking for and then set about achieving it. In the same way that you don't find a new place to live by not doing anything, nor can you expect your prince or princess to appear, as if by magic. If you do nothing but wait for Cupid, you could be waiting a long time, and you'll be absolving all responsibility – and power – you have.

Taking action does not mean rushing into the

first relationship that comes along. Nor does it mean that you settle for less than you want. 'There is only one real sin,' wrote the author, Doris Lessing 'and that is to persuade oneself that the second-best is anything but the second-best.'

Taking action means taking control, it means having a clear idea of what you want (and what you don't want) in a relationship. Always, it is better to focus on what you want rather than who you want. For example, wanting a relationship in which you both stay fit and healthy is better than wanting a partner who works out at the gym three times a week. Wanting to be with someone with whom you can develop your spiritual nature is more open-minded than wanting to be with someone of a specific faith or religion. When you know the basic things that you want and need and, at the same time, remain open-minded, you have a much greater chance of finding the right person.

For as many people as there are who want to find love and cannot, there are people who refuse to love because they feel that they cannot trust love. Maybe they fear love or feel undeserving in some way. Or maybe they've been deeply hurt and never again want to experience the pain of heartbreak. But if you cannot trust love, how can you get love? You can't. You need to be willing to take a chance, to learn to love again even when disappointment has hardened your heart, and your resolve. Great things always involve an element of risk. And there is no greater thing than love.

'Be friends first, lovers second, husband and wife third.' The advice of the teacher Torkom Saraydarian is perhaps more relevant today than it has ever been. Rising divorce rates, multiple partners and unhappy relationships all signify that we need guidance when it comes to trusting our precious heart to another.

Love, real love, doesn't happen like it does in the movies. We don't bump trolleys in the supermarket and are suddenly whisked off into some kind of starry fairytale in which we live happily ever after. Rarely do you hear of happily married couples for whom it was both love at first sight.

Because we live in an age of instant gratification, we expect everything immediately and if we don't get it immediately, we get frustrated. We have forgotten that some things cannot be hurried. We have lost awareness of the natural pace of things.

There is a natural pace at which you walk (although according to research, we are now even walking 10% faster than we did a decade ago). There is a natural pace at which a flower grows, a child learns, a cake is baked. Love has its own natural pace, and each love, a different pace. You cannot force love to blossom ahead of its time, nor neglect it by not bothering to water it with care and attention. In the same way that nature takes its own sweet time, so too does love.

Take your time to get to know someone well before you commit your heart to them. Far from being a waste of time, it enables you to discover if you both want the same things in a relationship. Most relationships fail because people want different things. If, by talking to each other, you discover that you are both looking for the same things, the relationship has a far more successful chance of working out.

Spending time with someone also allows you to pay attention to what they do, as well as what they say. Always, what we do reveals more about our true selves than what we say. And there is no other way to discover your true feelings for each other than to spend time together. We are complex, multi-layered beings, and we all want to protect our own private space. Only by communicating with each other, can we unwrap those layers and enter that private space, slowly, gently, and with utmost care and respect. You cannot do this with sex. You can only do this by talking. If you want to feel physically close to someone, hold them. Just holding someone helps the brain release the 'cuddle chemical' oxytocin, which induces feelings of warmth and love.

Of course, physical attraction is essential. If the attraction is not there, it's not there and time will not change that. Physical attraction is the glue that holds you together, but sex alone is not enough to sustain a relationship. Nor is friendship. You need, above all, to want the same or similar things, and be heading in the same direction.

Perhaps there is someone in your life with whom you are already good friends, someone who has the same values, and is looking for the same things. So often what – or who – we are searching for is right under our nose.

In love, as in life, everything changes. When you have found someone with whom you want to share your life, or at least part of your life, know that your relationship and your love will evolve and change, hopefully for the better. If though you find yourself – or your partner – changing in a way that hurts or doesn't feel comfortable, take care to watch what is happening. Don't dismiss your feelings as unimportant. Your feelings are always an accurate barometer of your thoughts. Trust your feelings, and honour your feelings. Is the relationship taking you closer to what you want? Or further away? Remember, you always have a choice and, having made a choice, you can always change your mind. That doesn't mean you give up at the first hurdle, it simply means that that you always consider what is best for you, and your partner. Love is not sacrificing yourself or your life to please another. Love is being true to yourself. When you are true to yourself, you can be true to another.

Staying in touch with your feelings is always a healthy thing to do. In the same way that a job review helps you focus on your strengths and weaknesses, a relationship review can do the same. When you take the time and awareness to think about how you feel, and where the relationship is heading, you are far better able to adjust to any changes that may be necessary. Are the two of you communicating as much as you'd like? Are you becoming too possessive? If so, know that you cannot own someone, and the more you trust someone, the less likely they are to make you question that trust. Nor can you change anyone, only yourself. Remember, it is often your differences that not only define you but which draw you to each other, and make you feel complete, like two sides of the same coin.

Remember too to give each other space, to 'let the winds of heaven dance between you,' as Kahil Gibran so poetically expressed.

Understanding that your relationship must change over time is crucial to long-term success. The sexual craving, elation and obsession that you feel when you first fall in love eventually give way to a steady emotional bond. This is when the in love becomes love. Passion becomes peace. Chaos becomes calm. Trembling becomes trust. And, as your heart of fire becomes a steady flame, its glow warming every aspect of your life, something deeper, more meaningful and infinitely more enduring is born.

As your love changes and grows, so too do you. Love is not always smooth sailing. Sometimes the sails fall flat and you feel like you're going nowhere. Sometimes the winds of change blow you temporarily off course. But if after a year, a decade or a century together, your heart still lifts when you hear your loved one's key in the door and if, when you think of each other, you still smile, and you are still true to each other and the dreams you share, then your love can ride any storm.

Keep the flame of your love alive. Look after your love. Happy ever after doesn't write itself, you write it together. You write it with every respectful word, every kind act, every generous thought. You watch your love like a mother watches her newborn child, caring for its every need. You disregard the small, unimportant things and give thanks for the things that count; the warm shelter of each other, the closeness, the comfort and laughter, the wonder of the world you have created, and the blessing that is your love.

SHINE

On one of the hottest days of summer in Sydney, a day on which even the parrots stopped squawking to rest in the dappled shade of the jacaranda trees, she sat, staring across the water and the tide that pulled back and pushed forward, back and forth, back and forth, a permanent reminder of the ebb and flow of life. And she found herself picking over the threads of the story of how she came to be here, and she cast her mind over all the experiences she had ever wanted, and those she did not, and how they were all a part of the adventure that was her life and how her life, this far, would be incomplete without them.

She had experienced passion, and savoured the bittersweet longing of unrequited love; she knew what it felt like to love someone who did not love her in return and, conversely, to be loved by one to whom she could never give her heart.

She knew what it was like to work with no sense of fulfilment, and to then discover the joy of work in which time itself stood still. She had strived to make her mark, and she had drunk from the cup of victory that was the reward for her efforts.

She had experienced the anguish of addiction in which she had soared to the highest heights and sunk to the deepest depths. She had done shameful things that had come from the weakness of her heart, and she had done brave and inspiring things that had demanded extraordinary strength and courage. She had fought her demons and she had won.

She had been blessed with the appreciation of wealth that comes from having gone without. And the appreciation of friendship that comes from having been lonely. She had garnered the riches of wisdom that comes from having made mistakes.

She had discovered the true meaning of things that can only be discovered by experiencing its opposite: that in pleasure there is pain, in darkness there is light, in sorrow there is joy, and in discipline there is freedom. With this discovery, she acquired a sense of balance in all things, and especially in herself.

She had fallen, in misery, on a stone cold floor, and lain on the desert stones gazing at the stars above her, in awe. She had found herself in the centre of the Universe, and had felt the Universe awaken in her.

She had nearly drowned, and been saved by an angel.

She had witnessed death, and suffered the pain

of separation and loss. And she had discovered the joy, the exquisite joy of love.

She had learned that the more she learned, the more there was still to learn. She had done all these things, and she had become all these things. And she arrived at a place where she felt the same but different. Where nothing and everything had changed.

In the beginning she had wanted to become someone more, to do something better, to create something that would make a difference to the world. She did not know then that this was the meaning of the journey – to become who she already was, to know herself, and to be changed for that.

She would never stop becoming, she would never stop growing, she was the architect of her own destiny, she thought as she recalled her mother's words 'you always have a choice', simply doing what she thought best at the time, trying to make the best decisions. 'Follow the light' her mother had also told her. Only now did she finally understand what her mother had meant, and what the light was that she must follow.

It was not the light of the sun that had led her to this faraway land. It was not the light that gleamed in the gold awards she had won, nor the spotlight of recognition that shined on her talent. The light was not the sparkling light of jewels on an exquisite dress that reflected her own shining beauty. It was not the burning light of desire in a lover's eyes, nor the glittering light of the chandelier that sparkled on the celebration of a marriage made and a friend found. And, though it took her breath away, the light was not the light of a million stars. It was not the light of candles glowing in a house of worship that comforted her in her time of loss. It was not even the eternal light of love, though she thought that this was perhaps the closest thing to it.

There had been times when she believed that each and every one of these things was the light that her mother had instructed her to follow. But now she knew that none of them was. She knew that the light was something else, something she could see only by looking in, not out.

The light was the light of her soul. It was the light she was born with and which accompanied her every step of her journey. And though at times the light was obscured behind a cloud of darkness, it could never be extinguished. Like a dancing flame, the light changed shape and colour, too, sometimes it was so small it was barely a flicker and at other times, when given just the briefest attention, it rose tall and bright.

She knew this light deserved her time and attention, not least because when she focussed on it, she was rewarded with an immediate and overwhelming sense of tranquillity and clarity of thinking, the benefits of which were immeasurable.

Sometimes, like this morning as she sat on the balcony overlooking the water and she was quiet and still, she closed her eyes and she could see the light and feel its warmth flooding through her very being and washing away any tension, soothing all sorrow. Penetrating and illuminating all corners, she could physically feel its rays shining through her and out of her, and she thought it felt like heaven. She never wanted to open her eyes, she never wanted to escape this ecstasy, this place where she wished for nothing and nothing troubled her.

She sensed things acutely; the sound of the chugging of a motorboat in the distance, the lapping of the water beneath the balcony, the dragonfly dancing across the surface of the water. She was stilled, silenced, agog, as if she were experiencing the world for the first time.

From the dirt road high above the boathouse, she heard the sound of Miguel's Kombi pulling up.

The engine stopped and the door slammed shut. And she heard his footsteps coming down the 101 stone steps towards her.

Slowly, she opened her eyes and her heart lifted, again, to the horizon, and the day.

SHINE

In your life you may search for what feels like an eternity to find what makes you happy. You can look for happiness all around you, and not find it. You can pack your bag and travel the world. You can chase after a shimmering thing in the distance that you believe is the answer to your dream and, when you get close, you can see that it is not what you thought it was but a mirage. And off you go again, to another place where you climb another mountain, take another job, find another bar, love another person, all the while looking for the elusive thing that will make you truly happy. At times it feels like the whole world is conspiring against you and you begin to think that the more you chase happiness, like a butterfly, the harder it is to catch. So, tired of disappointment, you stop searching.

Then, one day you're walking down the street or driving your car or watching the sun set, not thinking about anything in particular. And it comes to you, quietly, as all important realisations do; you feel happy. In this moment, in this place you feel this thing called happiness, this wonderful, light and warm feeling. And in the nanosecond that is a lifetime, you realise the truth; that happiness has never left you, it was with you all the time.

The source of true happiness can never be found by looking outside ourselves, only within. This is what the poet, T.S.Eliot meant when he wrote '... and the end of all our exploring will be to arrive where we started and know the place for the first time.'

True happiness, like true success, arrives without force or fanfare. In fact, that is the only time when it can arrive. Why? Because true happiness is the light of your soul shining through.

The truth that the happiness you seek lies within sounds so simple, yet it can take a lifetime to discover. So often the only way to learn about life is to explore life, and the only way to realise that happiness lies within is after you've looked for it elsewhere. For how else, if not by experience, can you learn that nothing and no-one can make you as happy as you. You, and only you, have control and power of your thoughts and feelings, and that includes happiness.

What you think always precedes what you do; your thoughts always become your experiences. There is no magic spell, no school of learning, nothing that can bring you closer to the happiness you want than you. So stop your chasing and stand still long enough to connect with yourself, and be what it is that you want to be. Just be it.

Be the happiness that is the light of your soul.

Know that all that you want is all that you have. All that you seek to discover, you already know. Everything you want to be, you already are. You are every footstep, every stumble, every mile you have walked that has led you here. You are every smile you have smiled, and every tear you have cried. You are every word you have spoken, every yes, and every no. You are every song you have sung and every dance you have danced. You are every kiss that has breathed love into your heart, and every hurt that has cut your heart in two. You are all your courage and compassion, all your strengths and your weaknesses. You are all your leaps of achievement and all your sighs of defeat. You are all your hopes, and all your fears. You are all that you have been, and all that you will be. You are not perfect. No-one is perfect. But it is your imperfections that make you the person that you are, and that is better than perfect.

Dream your dream. Big or small, your dream is the destination on the map that is your future. Without a dream, what is there to strive for?

Believe your dream will come true. Believe in miracles, and miracles will happen. Believe you will find love, and love will find you. Beyond believing, feel it. When you feel your dream coming true in vivid detail, your mind becomes focussed and helps you take action that supports your dream.

Strive to do your best, and don't be lazy. The easy way is not always the best way. If you are struggling and feel like you're getting nowhere, look to see if there is another path that will take you up the mountain.

Trust in the Universe. It has infinite power, more than enough to make your dreams come true.

Prosper. Whatever you give your time, your attention and your heart to will magnify tenfold. Be generous, and your generosity will be rewarded in ways you cannot begin to imagine. When you understand that, in life, you get what you give, you come to realise that there is no limit to the abundance of riches – physical, emotional and spiritual – that are yours.

Balance. In between fast and slow, high and low, lies the point of perfect equilibrium. When you find that point of balance, you find the stability that is at the very core of you, and you develop poise and a presence in which all things happen in perfect timing.

Desire is a human emotion, but so often what we desire or want is not good for us. There are many occasions when it's better not to act on your desires. When you find the strength to walk away from your desires, the most amazing thing happens. You become more discriminating, desiring only that which is truly valuable, and worth investing your precious time, energy or money. And because you give yourself to what is really special, you get back what is special.

Accept the place you are at right now. Accept it all, the good and the bad. Only when you are completely honest with yourself and accepting of all that is real, can you make the decision to change yourself, and your situation. Acceptance always comes before change. And when you embrace change, instead of resisting change, life immediately becomes less of a battle.

Choose to act and respond at all times and to all situations in the way that fits with the highest vision you have of yourself. This takes discipline, but when you do this, the rewards are instantaneous. Set yourself standards and a code of behaviour that works for you, not against you. When you take the time to consider the consequences of your actions, you take control of your life, and your future.

Heal your body and you will go much further, much faster. You cannot drive a broken car very far, nor can you live well on a broken body. Understand that your mind, body and spirit are inextricably linked, and that if you neglect one, all suffer. Your healing begins with your spirit. Be guided by a strong moral compass and you will find it easier to become emotionally, mentally and physically strong.

Connect with your world and everything in it. In spite of all you see in the news, there is much goodness and beauty around you. Add your own goodness and beauty to the world. Always, the way you treat others is the way you treat yourself. Take what you need and give what you can. Be kind. We're all in this together, we're all trying to get on, to make our dreams come true. Your dreams are important, but no more or less important than those of the person standing next to you.

Endure your trials. Life doesn't always turn out in the way you want, and never in the way that you expect. Your challenges are given to you for a reason, though that reason may not seem clear (and definitely not fair) at the time. During hard times, be gentle with yourself and surround yourself with gentle people. Know that, as surely as sunshine follows rain, difficult days will pass.

Let go of ideas, habits and things that do not serve you well. Let go, too, of people who prevent you being true to yourself or who, by being with you, cannot be true to themselves. Life is precious and short, too short for regrets.

Be in this moment, and all that is supporting you in this moment; the air that you breathe and the ground beneath you. Be still enough to find yourself, to connect with the light of your soul, and you will find yourself in a place that is impervious to everyday worries, a place that gives you comfort, strength and healing and which will nurture you through all situations, and all times.

Love yourself as much as you love others. Love what it is that makes you unique and special. When you love, you are free and there are no boundaries, no limits to what you can feel and can do. Not things, not money, only love is real. Only love never dies.

Shine your light, the bright, burning, infinite light of your soul; the light that shows you the way, that guides you and gives you hope, faith and purpose.

There will be times when the light is hidden by a veil of illusion, but it is still there. There will be times when the light is dimmed by the storms of defeat and despair, but it is still there. The light can never be extinguished. Because you are the light. The light is you.

Shine the light that you are. Shine inside and out. Shine all day and all night. Shine through the clouds and the rain. Shine. And the world will bask in the warmth of your light.

BIBLIOGRAPHY

Barack Obama speech after Super Tuesday primaries, February 2008.

Linus from Peanuts by Charles M Schulz.

Charles, Prince of Wales, from The Passionate Prince, BBC, broadcast BBC1, 12 November 2008.

Paulo Coelho, Manual of the Warrior of Light, Harper Collins, 2002.

Torkom Saraydarian, Dynamics of Success, TSG Publishing Foundation, 1992.

Marianne Williamson, Everyday Grace, Bantam Books, 2002.

Magic Penny by Malvina Reynolds, copyright 1955 and 1958 Northern Music Corporation.

Inner Workings of the Magnanimous Mind by Dr Jorge Moll for National Institute of Neurological Studies, April 2007.

Torkom Saraydarian, Aura, Shield of Protection & Glory, TSG Publishing Foundation, Inc.

John O'Donohue. Divine Beauty, The Invisible Embrace. Published by Bantam Press 2004. Reprinted by permission of The Random House Group Limited.

Thich Nhat Hanh, www.plumvillage.org

Neale Donald Walsh. Conversations with God, Hodder & Stoughton 1995.

Dalai Lama. 20 Ways to Get Good Karma, Instructions for Life. Wisdom Articles, 16 November 2006. www.spiritualnow.com

Billie Jean King from 'Wisdom: 50 Unique and Original Portraits by Andrew Zuckerman, Abrams, 2008.

Sol Luckman, The Biology of Enlightenment, Sol Luckman, 2005.

Magnetic by Wendy Cope, Ten Poems about Love, Candlestick Press, 2008.

Bill Clinton interview by Alan Rusbridger and Jonathan Freedland, The Guardian, 21 June 2004.

Eisabeth Kübler-Ross, On Life After Death, Celestial Arts, 1991. Reprinted by arrangement with The Elisabeth Kübler-Ross Family LP and The Barbara Hogenson Agency. All rights reserved. For more information, visit: www.EKRFoundation.org

Deepak Chopra, Life After Death, Rider Books, 2006.

HH Dalai Lama and Howard C Cutler, The Art of Happiness, Hodder & Stoughton, 1998.

Ekhart Tolle, Stillness Speaks, Hodder and Stoughton, 2003.

Ohiyesa (Dr. Charles Eastman), Santee Sioux, And Wisdom Comes Quietly, Exley Publications, 2000.

The National Academies of Sciences, published 10 August 08, Sara Lazard, Harvard University as part of Kavli Frontiers of Science Symposium.

'Letting Mind Clear Improves Attention Span.' The New York Times, May 20, 2007.

Pierre Pradervant, The Gentle Art of Blessing, Cygnus Books, 2003.

I've been high by R.E.M. on Reveal, Warner Bros. Records Inc. 2001.

Dalai Lama on Love and Compassion. www.brainyquote.com

'Speed of Walkers' by Professor Richard Wiseman, University of Hertfordshire.

Kahil Gibran, The Prophet.

T.S. Eliot, Little Gidding.

Lightning Source UK Ltd.
Milton Keynes UK
UKOW041144051212

203220UK00002B/379/P